Donna Henningson offers us a highly creative and original way to think and dream about conflict. She kept me guessing and engaged all along the learning journey.

—Matthew Legge, Psychology Today blogger, and award-winning author of *Are We Done Fighting? Building Understanding in a World of Hate and Division* (2019)

THOUGHTS FROM THE BENCHES

Over 18 seasons, **Fred Harbinson (President/ General Manager/ Head Coach)** has led the Penticton Vees of the British Columbia Hockey League (BCHL) to 18 various championship titles across the region, province, western division, and nationally. Harbinson has been the BCHL's coach of the year four times, most recently in 2021-22.

The Penticton Vees may be a small-town hockey team, but their reputation is far from small. In 1955, the Vees (named after three local varieties of peaches: victory, valiant, vidette), defeated the Russians at the amateur World Hockey Championships (watch the game at www.greatesthockey-legends.com). The Vees led the British Columbia Hockey League (BCHL) in a 2012 record-setting championship run, as well as topping the league in 2015, 2017, 2022 and 2023. (The COVID-19 pandemic prevented playoffs in 2020 and 2021).

"Every team no matter how successful has internal conflict," Harbinson says. "In fact, the best teams – championship teams for that matter – are the ones that don't fear conflict. The fear of conflict can paralyze a team. My teams have always embraced conflict by expressing to the individual or individuals that there is a genuine care and concern for their argument/position.

"Even though they don't always get what they want, by showing that you respect their opinion and that it's not the old 'my way or the highway' you can create a buy-in that will help solve your conflict more times than not, and galvanize your team in the process."[1]

General Manager Larry Pidperyhora Jr's Penticton Toyota car dealership went up in flames 4:30 a.m. May 11, 2022, in a massive fire that brought out approximately 25 firefighters, destroyed much inventory, and gutted the shop and service bays. The showroom and main structure were saved. A local man was charged with arson and mischief over $5,000.

Interviewed at the time of the fire, Pidperyhora spoke of the devastation of his dealership team (which he described as being "like a family"). He spoke of the outpouring of support from the community including industry colleagues. With mop-up operations ongoing, the team set up temporary operating practices. "Assume the worst," Pidperyhora said, "and then hopefully be surprised with something better."

A year later, he said, "All in all, we are people dealing with people. I feel that everyone wants an amicable environment to exist at all times. Empathy is probably one of the most powerful tools we can deploy when faced with conflict. It takes a cognizant effort to be empathetic, and that pause often gives us enough time to centre ourselves to a goal of achieving a desired outcome.

"It can be easy to take offense, or get into defensive positions when faced with conflict, but again - with that empathetic pause - it can shift the dynamic quickly from adversarial to collaborative, which ultimately will get things done positively and effectively.

"This has been our mantra as we moved through the drama of our business burning down, to grinding through the rebuild."[2]

White Space, Gray Areas & Black Swans

stories of getting along (or not)

Donna M. Henningson

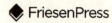
FriesenPress

One Printers Way
Altona, MB R0G 0B0
Canada

www.friesenpress.com

Copyright © 2024 by Donna M. Henningson
First Edition — 2024

All rights reserved.

No part of this publication may be reproduced in any form, or by any means, electronic or mechanical, including photocopying, recording, or any information browsing, storage, or retrieval system, without permission in writing from FriesenPress.

This is a creative work of nonfiction. Nonetheless, some of the names and personal characteristics of the individuals involved have been changed in order to disguise their identities. Any resulting resemblance to persons living or dead is entirely coincidental and unintentional.

Courtesy of the author: front cover images (Skaha Lake, Penticton, B.C.; black swan). Also dedication haiku poem.

https://dmhenningson.ca
donnahenningson@gmail.com

ISBN
978-1-03-830332-5 (Hardcover)
978-1-03-830331-8 (Paperback)
978-1-03-830333-2 (eBook)

1. Young Adult Nonfiction, Diversity & Multicultural

Distributed to the trade by The Ingram Book Company

For Alan
with love always.
Following, I steer
windblown, haunted, but hopeful.
No path, but to live.

FOREWORD

One evening in the early stages of writing this book I was making research notes. I got up from my kitchen table laptop - binders and papers spread around me - and walked into another room to get yet more notes.

I'd been thinking how big this writing project had become. Eight months prior, it was to be a straightforward personal essay to work through some conflict resolution issues for myself.

But now it looked like a book project. Though years before I'd been a full-time print journalist at a community daily newspaper, I'd never written a book. This particular evening the weight of it was heavy and I felt overwhelmed. Will it ever end? With a sigh I turned to go back to my laptop.

As I did, I saw a small stack of papers on the bookshelf. Great! Forgot about those. Then my eye caught sight of a couple of small-sized sheets of phone messages in my handwriting stapled together and sitting at the front of the stack.

I glanced through them, and saw "Dad" written next to a comment hidden under the staple. Curious, I pried underneath: "'8:09 pm Tues. You got to forget things and start anew' 'Sat. Dad - apologize anything I said to you' '8:06pm Tues Aug 2? Dad - apologize for anything I did.'"

I gaped at the words. Was it a phone message he'd left years ago? A few minutes before, I was reading about what it means to forgive. And now my gentle Dad's words were here in front of me.

He'd been dead for seven years.

I couldn't quite place the context, some long-forgotten disagreement. We'd long since moved on from it and reconciled. But it showing up at that moment was startling. My writing project was taking up most of my time and attention, hunkered over the keyboard for hours, reading what popular thought leaders were saying about leadership and conflict resolution. Trying to regain a sense of personal control.

And here was my dad in total character telling me from the grave, "Hey, don't take things so seriously. Let it go. You've got to move on." In my mind's eye the warmth of his easy-going presence filled the room. In effect he was saying to not expect too much from my project. I may not get the answers I wanted. And that's okay. This is life, it's a mystery and there's more important ways to spend my precious time.

My takeaway was, if I'm to learn anything from this project, it's how to get good at working with friction and conflict for the good of all, at not taking situations, events, actions too seriously, too personally. And get on with life.

Thanks, Dad. xxoo

Donna M. Henningson
Summerland
Wednesday, April 27, 2022

TABLE OF CONTENTS

Thoughts From the Benches	*iii*
Foreword	*viii*
Note to Reader	*xii*
Introduction	*xiii*
Characters	*xvii*

PART ONE - FAMOUS OR UNSUNG

Chapter One - Coming Together	**3**
Driving to the Queen E	3
Four Guys	7
Chapter Two - Culture Speaks	**14**
Back To The Beginning	14
Culture Warp	17
Crossing Oceans And Crossing Paths	20
Himalayan Women Making It Work	26
Mongol Queens	32
China's Last Matriarchy	38
Three Destinies	46
Survival of The Useful: Ice Age Tips	46
Academic – Activist – Artist	48
Marketplace Mojo: Tall Again in The Saddle	53
Mojag Hijinks with Justin and Jody	59
Chapter Three -Everyday Aggravation	**65**
The Big "Try" - Walking Them In	65
Teacher Rumble	69
Grand Tour	77
Sports, Slaps, and Feeling Like a Woman	82

PART TWO - MIND, EMOTION & SPIRIT

"Tip Talk" Forum	93
Chapter One - Mind	***96***
Flowered Dress: Can I Trust You?	96
Silky: Youth Meets Age-Old Wisdom	102
Chapter Two - Emotion	***110***
Leadership and Courage: The Emotional Cliff	110
Chapter Three - Spirit	***122***
Confidence in Inner Spirit	122
Bigger Than Me	127

PART THREE – SPEAKING IN BLACK SWAN

Black Swan Soars	134
Afterword	138
Acknowledgements	***144***
Index	***146***
Endnotes	***163***

NOTE TO READER

How have others around the world in different cultures and periods of time managed to get along?

Our three characters - White Space (WSpace), Gray Area (GArea), and Black Swan (BSwan) - must consider multicultural stories of interpersonal challenges, and answer that question. Time is running out. There's a big gathering coming up. They need to prepare.

WSpace, GArea and BSwan are hopeful. They have faith that one or more of these tales will mean something to you the reader in your own life story.

-*Donna M. Henningson (author)*

INTRODUCTION

WSpace stands hunched over the sink, the ceiling light swaying just barely on its thin cord throwing a warm glow over her auburn curls pulled back and tied in a pony tail. Methodically she shifts from silverware to dishes, the dingy water sloshing in the basin. She's hunkered over the tougher pots and pans, her muscles straining.

She's a slight-built woman in her early 50s, short, lean without an extra ounce of body fat, her facial features and cheekbones etched prominently, a marathon runner in her spare time. She glides silently from side to side retrieving a dish here a glass there.

Finally, she wipes the counters clear with her cloth, the surfaces gleaming, and sighs. Getting the dishes done and out of the way each night always gives her room to breathe.

At the kitchen table GArea, a stodgy older man in his mid-70s, shifts in his chair and grunts, his head buried in a plume of smoke behind the day's newspaper. He's medium height with drooping jowls and a big belly. GArea has put on a few pounds over the years. He wears faded casual, loose jeans and thick gray wavy hair nearing his shoulders. "How the hell they gonna do that?" he mutters to himself about the day's headlines. "They've no idea how it works or how to find out. Caught up in their own LaLa Lands."

He hoists himself up stiffly, shuffles past WSpace over to the coffee pot in the corner, and pours himself a mugful. "Looks like we've got our work cut out for us with this one," he addresses her and she nods absently.

"BSwan doesn't want anything to eat?" she asks catching his eye. "I swear They eat like a bird." BSwan announced earlier that month totally without warning that "They" had decided to forego binary gender pronouns. Though the other two meant well, they often forgot. Once, in the middle of a video conference BSwan slipped GArea a tiny piece of paper that read "They, Them, Their." GArea got the message.

BSwan is down in the basement, doing what BSwan does best: being mysterious. BSwan is tall, long-limbed, good-looking in Their late 20s. Today BSwan is in the usual gear: court shoes, a drab-coloured old T-shirt and sweat pants. Long strands of tousled dark hair fall constantly across dark eyes hidden behind dark-rimmed glasses. BSwan is usually either deep in thought, internet browsing, or texting.

Strains of a pop hit from the 1960s about being misunderstood drift up the stairs. WSpace and GArea had long since learned that BSwan would appear when the time came, and not a minute before.

"Is the drone ready?" GArea asks WSpace, the two of them each grabbing a coat, hat, and scarf, then a briefcase stuffed full with binders, file folders, books and papers. "Yes!" she calls, before yelling forcefully down the stairs, "Swan! If you're coming, grab your stuff now and get up here. We're leaving!" The two head out the door into the night, a howling wind greeting them.

From the basement the music stops, replaced by a flurry of activity.

* * *

The drone is particularly large. Or the three of them are particularly small, depending on your perspective. How to explain their travel by drone over time and space? It just is. The drone moves back and forth over the years as easily as it dips and swerves between objects. Magical, mysterious, the drone's window on humankind lights up a dizzying variety of perspectives and viewpoints.

The team's role is less to argue a viewpoint, than it is to together observe the nuances of human behavior and compare impressions. As such, WSpace, GArea and BSwan aren't debaters. The three drone team-members sit at a horseshoe-shaped table, peering out the drone's front cockpit into the inky night, the whir of the electronics barely audible as the drone soars high over the miles and years dropping away below. Material from the briefcases lays scattered on the table between them.

Where the drone team comes from, and who they work for are also a mystery. The drone team has not so much been chosen for any expertise, but randomly selected from the general public, much like a trial jury.

WSpace runs marathons in her spare time. As a hobby, GArea plays guitar in a 70's retro rock band. BSwan loves to cook.

The three aren't conflict experts but fairly ordinary citizens from across a wide geographic area. Any person faces similar challenges in getting along with others. Like anyone, the drone team has strengths and weaknesses, and potential. Nothing in particular sets WSpace, GArea and BSwan apart from anyone else. What each of them does for a living is beside the point. How they each interact with other people is pretty typical. That's just how it is.

Previously they'd worked together a few times and gotten into a rhythm. They themselves don't know much about the people leading the project. The project leaders don't represent countries, organizations, or particular philosophies, so these leaders can work closely with a broad cross-section of cultures.

There are some people who reveal very little about themselves. WSpace is one of them. She is an observant, thoughtful woman of few spoken words or expressed emotions. Neither GArea nor BSwan have seen her lose her temper. She's silent when others vent, providing balance and waiting out the storm of emotions around her. That's her power. She works hard in the background, the rock of the team. WSpace had once likened their work to uncovering the pieces of a puzzle, and both GArea and BSwan nodded in agreement. It's satisfying, she says, to put the pieces of interpersonal communication together in a way that helps everyone, instead of the few (if that ever really is true).

Back where she comes from (apparently somewhere in North America), there's a daughter, but neither GArea or BSwan have heard her mention a husband, a partner.

As for GArea, he's always on the lookout to delve deeper, ask more questions, and even be a bit crochety, wondering why others are the way they are. He signs on to the drone expeditions again and again, apparently thrilled to play a part. His background is also unknown. He may have adult kids and grandkids somewhere, or be a widower, but he has never talked of his personal life.

While WSpace is often silent in the background, GArea is up front. He doesn't hesitate to voice his opinion and speak his mind. He's not very diplomatic, whereas WSpace often plays that role. It isn't wise to get in GArea's way. He can be difficult to deal with, but at his core he's dedicated to the cause of cooperation. Though he appears to be in constant complaint mode, his heart is good and he pitches in where he can once he's pointed in the right direction.

Then there's BSwan representing younger thought though not always. BSwan is a bit of an "old soul," a younger sibling, and a big reader. BSwan sits hunched in a chair, unassuming, making sense of the surrounding situation, watching and waiting for WSpace and GArea to take the lead. At the same time, BSwan is an astute student of human interaction and full of surprises.

Life is a mystery. So are life's teammates, and that's the way it is on this drone. WSpace, GArea and BSwan have different takes on any situation. For this assignment, they're considering stories of ordinary people, famous people, thought leaders, and people from various cultures, various times. What can be learned from them?

The ultimate question is always the same: How can we get along for the good of all involved? The drone lights dim. WSpace, GArea, and BSwan sit poised - pens, pencils and markers in hand, phones and laptops at the ready - and wait expectantly for the first story to begin.

CHARACTERS

WHITE SPACE (WSpace): [1] a phrase from graphic design practice (ie the empty parts between the painted bits); silence; physical distance; time to consider; neutral zone; time out; "Give me some room here!"; "You're crowding me!"; "You're sucking the air out of the room!"

GRAY AREA (GArea): [2] confusion; what's right and wrong is unclear (who are the good guys? the bad guys?); go slow to go fast (and get it right); what's been overlooked? undervalued?; interpretations differ; not obvious; blind spot; see two viewpoints at once; question; investigate; see irony, paradox; "What do you mean by that?"

BLACK SWAN (BSwan): [3] life is random and out of human control; an unexplained event, action, outcome unanticipated by some people but not necessarily all people; unique; not expected; powerful; unable to estimate impact of it; misunderstood

WSpace (neutral zone) + GArea (fill in gaps) = BSwan (unique)

PART ONE -
Famous or Unsung

CHAPTER ONE -
Coming Together

Granddaughter vowed to never, ever do such a thing again. Never force a resolution between two people when they aren't ready. Never compromise people's trust in her that way.

DRIVING TO THE QUEEN E

PREVIEW:

1. Have you ever tried to force people to get along? How well did it work?

2. When you see two people who aren't getting along, is there anything you can do to improve the situation? Explain.

* * *

De-cluttering her crawlspace, Granddaughter found a 1989 receipt from a flower shop.

Her Grandmother had bought red and white carnations and sent them to her Mother with the note "In gratitude…with Love." A scribbled note on the back of the receipt read, "She brought back these flowers to me. This is what she did to her mother, she has a cold, cold heart…. Shame… 1989 year."

Odd. Grandmother was the one with the reputation for shutting people out, leaving them scratching their heads. She'd done it with others. Granddaughter didn't know the details.

Granddaughter also didn't know details of the rift between her gentle Mother, and volatile Grandmother. Back then, Granddaughter only knew that her Mother apparently refused to see Grandmother. The gift of flowers was a gesture that didn't come easy to Grandmother: opening herself, making herself vulnerable. If Mother returned the flowers, it must have felt like a very painful slap in the face. The door slammed shut.

At one point Granddaughter had tried to bring the two older women together, forced the matter. Told both that Granddaughter was taking them to a play at the Queen Elizabeth Theatre in Vancouver. Didn't say the other was coming, too. Granddaughter and Mother headed off for the hour-long drive downtown. Granddaughter took a 30-minute detour and picked up Grandmother, who took this to mean all was well. But Mother was horrified, and sat in silence.

They got to the Queen E. Granddaughter realized it wasn't going to work, and suggested they go for coffee. The three sat in silence at a nearby restaurant. Grandmother leaned forward, trying to make conversation. In front of her on the other side of the table, Mother was totally silent. Granddaughter took them both home, defeated.

Grandmother later told Granddaughter she didn't sleep that night, she was so upset.

Granddaughter vowed to never, ever do such a thing again. Never force a resolution between two people when they aren't ready. Never compromise people's trust in her that way. Grandmother and Mother were still estranged when Grandmother died in 1999 at the age of 90.

Reconciliation is not easy. Generally, people know it's important. But it challenges everything we are, and the basis of our relationships.

How to get better at defusing friction before the need for reconciliation? How to get better at conflict resolution, mediation, and leadership? Just who is "at fault" in any one situation becomes murky and almost beside the point. It becomes less important to pinpoint fault, than to focus on the process of getting along to move forward (in spiritual writer Marianne Williamson's words, the "mysterious river").[1]

* * *

GArea leans back in his chair. "Hm, family. Definitely one of the toughest." With a distant look, WSpace cups her chin in one hand. In a dark corner, BSwan has a drink of water.

WSpace: "Granddaughter found the flower shop receipt years later, so she didn't know about the Flowers Return, when she did the Drive."

GArea: "Mute point. The Drive wasn't a smart move."

BSwan: "Like, she was hoping for a Quick Fix, okay? But no one had done the Homework, ya?"

The three sit in silence.

WSpace: "Granddaughter showed a lot of courage. Remember, she's the young one, and not even really sure of what the Fight was about."

GArea: "So what's the lesson? You should know better than any of us, that she needed to take the time to find out what the Fight was about."

WSpace: "Ya, true. What would that have looked like? She needed to sit her mother and grandmother down separately and give each of them time to express their feelings, point of view."

GArea: "Right. This couldn't be a spur of the moment thing."

BSwan: "No, and even then there was no guarantee the Drive would have produced any breakthrough, right?"

GArea: "During the Drive, it was the mom in particular who totally shut down. The granddaughter really jeopardized trust there."

WSpace: "Uh-huh. Though the grandmother was upset about the flowers, she seemed to be willing to put it behind her, and talk together. Really quite excited about it."

GArea: "Ya, a bit out of character, but a good lesson too, that - depending on the situation - some of the toughest nuts to crack can actually be the pussycats, to mix metaphors."

WSpace smiles: "So, more time needed to pull each aside separately to listen for positions, needs. Time to consider."

BSwan, feet crossed on a hassock, twirls a pen between two fingers: "Ya, and probably floating the idea of the Drive in advance between the two. Sort of, giving them time to think about it, right?"

GArea: "They may not have agreed, especially the mom, but that's the chance the granddaughter takes. It's not her call. She needed to have the others have some say." He leans back, his hands behind his head, and gives a laugh. "Much less risky as far as jeopardizing trust. Who knows what that granddaughter would try next?"

WSpace leans forward and gives GArea a deep look: "She meant well."

The three close the file, and prepare for the next story. BSwan gives a yawn. GArea is still thinking about the ill-fated drive to the Queen E, not quite ready to let it go.

GArea: "But good intentions just don't cut it, to have people get along. Good intentions alone are just a waste of time and effort." As they are talking, the drone had already been gently vibrating, making headway to their next destination.

BSwan is ready to move on: "Awesome! What's next? Those four guys?" The others nod.

* * *

REVIEW:

1. How would you have handled the situation, if you were the grand-daughter? The mother? The grandmother?

2. What is a "core value"? What is the granddaughter's core value? Choose one, and explain your choice: 1) theatre 2) family 3) time together, or?

Our actions affect others, and none of us know in advance which actions.

FOUR GUYS

PREVIEW:

1. Which would you rather be: a) famous by yourself, or b) famous as a group? Explain.
2. How important is a sense of humour to get along with others?

* * *

Taking the Bus

The story goes that, despite his wealth and fame, one day Paul McCartney took the double-decker public bus that ran from his posh home in north London past the Twickenham studio where the Beatles were recording at the time.

In January 1969, McCartney and Beatles bandmates John Lennon, George Harrison, and Ringo Starr were aiming to write 14 songs in three weeks (first at Twickenham, then Apple Corp studios) for what would be the "Let It Be" album.[1]

McCartney had been disguising his appearance to get from street level to studio without being recognized. But, on this day, the bus conductor recognized and scolded him. Public transit, the driver insisted, wasn't for privileged people like Paul McCartney. The irony is striking.[2]

In 1968, McCartney wrote the song "Blackbird" in reaction to 1960s racial strife in the U.S. South. The simple act of taking the local public bus got both Paul McCartney of the most famous pop band in the world in trouble, and – at least a decade and an ocean apart - Black American civil rights activist Rosa Parks.[3]

One bus incident was a relatively minor inconvenience for McCartney to do with privilege and class politics (for once away from the public eye).

The other was Parks getting arrested in an ongoing series of planned non-violent protest actions. This particular refusal to give up her seat, however, would go down in history for gaining much sympathy during the Civil Rights movement. The backlash would create employment problems for Parks and her family for years to come.[4]

Actions affect others, and no one knows in advance which actions. Taking the bus is a great equalizer, rubbing shoulders with all kinds of people. Some resent taking the bus as a necessity, and see it as a symbol of low status, as just being one of the masses.

Others, like McCartney, see the chance to be "just one of the masses" as a release that grounds him, reassuring him he's still himself, still "ordinary." He says he still enjoys taking a bus. Once in New York, he got on and it appeared clear all recognized him, but didn't say or do anything.

All but a Black woman in the back who in a loud voice asked if he was Paul McCartney (he confirmed it), and why he was on that bus. He invited her to sit next to him. They shared where they were going (she uptown to see her sister), and had what he later called a "lovely" conversation.[5]

Four British teenagers, one dream – to make it big. In the late 1950's, John had started a band. Then he met Paul through a friend. Paul had noticed John on the public Liverpool bus off and on, and was taken with his "Teddy Boy" style popular at the time.[6]

Both wrote songs, though neither could read or write music. Paul later brought George (the youngest in the band), who would become their "incredible technician."[7]

While hired to play in Hamburg, Germany, John, Paul, George and drummer Pete Best met drummer Richard Starkey ("Ringo Starr"), who had more experience performing. As a result, Best's Beatles days were numbered.[8]

The other four got together and eventually caught the eye of industry insiders, then exploded onto the British and American pop music scene in early 1964 as Beatlemania. But behind the mass hysteria were months of daily eight-hour performance bookings. Learning together. Getting into a groove.[9]

In the drone, White Space, Gray Area, and Black Swan had been eating toast while watching the Beatles story unfold out the window. GArea belches, then reaches for a tooth pick. "Poor kids make good. End of story."

"Well, actually," WSpace gives him a look, "John came from a fairly well-to-do family."

BSwan leans forward: "Like, kids getting together is not so special. They're all from Liverpool. You know but apart from Paul and George who were already friends, they could just as easily have never crossed paths."

GArea cuts in, "We could argue that all day. The musician community of a certain age must have been fairly small."

"Okay let's not get into it," BSwan sighs. "This particular foursome met and made a band. Kind of their own 'circle of safety' against the world. They were like so many other kids of the time with stars in their eyes, you know?" [10]

Keeping It Ordinary

Suddenly BSwan smirks, a gleam in the eye. "Oh my god, but take a look at that early 'working it' video, whatever it's called. It's really awesome! Very candid. Personalities quite different from each other."[11]

The mothers of both Paul and John died when the boys were still teens. Paul's mom died from breast cancer when Paul was 14; John's mom was run over by an off-duty police officer when John was 17. [12] In the video, the four come across as approachable, ordinary. Candid, without a put-on performance "game face."

BSwan appears smitten. "Paul is so cute singing melody to the camera, you know! He's the band heartthrob. John sort of hams it up at the keyboard next to him and Paul kind of glances at him, hehe. Oh ya, George studies his own fingers, and mouths the guitar chords to himself like he's just learned them. The camera doesn't linger on him. At one point, George just sits down to get more comfortable. Ringo seems like he's ready to fall asleep at any moment."

WSpace leans on one hand, and smiles. "It's like they're saying, hey we're just like all of you kids! Really quite striking."

Recording at the time was relatively primitive, and they created songs they could memorize, geared to the tastes of their target audience (young people who were like them). Later, they would get more experimental. [13]

Paul told talk show host Larry King in 2002, that what set them apart was they were "artsy." John had been an arts student. Paul had studied A-Level literature: Shakespeare, Chaucer. The Lennon/McCartney combo was special, he told King, while George and Ringo were very good musicians. Ringo was low maintenance, and didn't have to be cued. It all just clicked. [14]

GArea taps a pen on the table to a rhythm known only to him: "While in this routine of Lennon and McCartney writing songs, they make it very big. They seem to have a winning formula. Why change?"

Fanning the Flame

The Fab Four learn early how fame and stardom come with a price. You think it's tough sometimes to work together as a band? Multiply that by a massive audience base, each fan with their own life experiences, beliefs and opinions.

Some of their fans didn't like Ringo taking over from Pete Best as drummer. In August 1962, after Pete's last performance with the Beatles and Ringo's first appearance, fans of Pete held vigils outside Pete's house, shouting a chant in his favor. One upset fan gives George a black eye, and band manager Brian Epstein hires George a bodyguard.[15]

BSwan pauses, deep in thought, and lets a silence take hold. "Like, that adoration, that unpredictable energy, would get much more disturbing, you know, and much more difficult to predict, to prepare for."

Over the years, the band dynamic shifted. Epstein, the father figure, died. Paul appeared to step in to fill the void. George showed his own talent as a songwriter, and resented not being taken more seriously, not being included more in later albums. In early 1969, he threatened to leave. Ringo watched it all unfold from his drum set.[16]

In 1966 before a U.S. tour, an off-hand comment by John in a British interview that the Beatles were "...more popular than Jesus," would ignite a firestorm in the U.S. bible belt, and fears for the band's safety. John apologized for the "Jesus" comment. At one point during the tour, someone in the audience threw a firecracker on stage. It exploded sounding like gunfire. The Beatles gave up live performance. "John himself was triggered by what he saw as mindless mob attitude, whether it was from Beatles fans, or religious dogma." GArea swivels to address WSpace and BSwan. "It was a definite theme in some later songs." The Beatles split up in 1970. In 1980, John and wife Yoko Ono were returning to their New York apartment building after a recording session. A self-professed "Christian" upset with John's caustic lyrics shot him. John died later in hospital of his injuries. He was 40 years old.[17]

"He was driven to keep poking the bear." BSwan shifts to face GArea.

"Until finally the bear strikes back," WSpace murmurs sadly.

Ono continued to live at the Dakota until 2023, when she reportedly moved to a farm she bought years before with John.[18]

GArea's head is bent. He keeps his eyes on the floor as he speaks softly. "John was a lightning rod, for better or worse."

"He found a way to stand out." WSpace rests a hand on GArea's arm. "And he did."

Bonding as Brothers, Pushing the Limits

Back in 1969, the Beatles had become an industry that needed constant feeding. The push was to get another creative album success, "as if the biggest band in the world or their handlers had a momentum problem," BSwan breaks in. "If they didn't keep kind of pushing themselves, they or their fans might sort of lose interest or just plain burn out, you know?"

Epstein, EMI producer George Martin, and keyboardist Billy Preston had made substantial contributions. Would it be enough to maintain the Beatles machine? Not everyone in the band was for a concert on the roof of the Apple Corps studio at 3 Savile Row in the heart of central London's office and fashion district. When the day came for the unpublicized noon-hour event January 30, 1969, Paul was still for it, but Ringo had misgivings citing the cold January weather. George wasn't particularly interested. According to "Let It Be" documentary director Michael Lindsay-Hogg, present at the time, George had usually been easy to get along with, but had become more difficult. It took John to commit to taking yet another risk, what would be the Beatles' last public performance: "F**k it, let's do it." [19]

The new manager Allen Klein re-negotiated a Beatles contract with Apple Corp September 1, 1969. A month later, John said he was leaving the band. But it was Paul who made it legal a year later on December 31, 1970 by filing suit to formally dissolve the Beatles partnership. The Beatles had been a band 10 years, and they were still in their 20's. It would take another four years to formally end the business, and be released from recording obligations.[20]

"They were growing up, getting married, having kids." WSpace lists the intrusions on one hand. "And they were making A LOT of money, more than they ever imagined. Priorities changed." GArea raises a finger and

PART ONE - FAMOUS OR UNSUNG

his eyebrows to also remind the other two, "John was excited about a new manager, but the others weren't."

GArea, WSpace and BSwan decide to finish for the evening, and resume at first light. They crawl into their separate pods, and pull down the shade screens. Soon the room is dark and silent except for the hum of the drone.

In 1971, John told talk show host Dick Cavett the Beatles were losing steam. Their wives weren't to blame. Paul told talk show host Larry King in 2002, that tensions over the new manager put their friendship under strain.[21]

While John had criticized Paul in public, Paul later told 60 Minutes Australia that he himself didn't criticize John in public, and Paul was glad. Eventually, Paul felt he'd made his peace with John prior to John's death. John was John, Paul said, and tended to fool around. You couldn't take it personally.[22]

In 1971, George told Cavett that George had been frustrated at how few of his songs were included in their albums. He started songwriting, he said, to break in on the Lennon-McCartney success.[23] When George walked out during the 1969 studio sessions, it was later at Ringo's house where they all met to hash over issues.

Ringo told talk show host Stephen Colbert in March 2021 that his own attitude from his perch at the drum-kit was to be prepared, watch the others, and contribute where needed: "I'm right with you, brother." For Ringo as an only child, the others mattered. There was strife. But there was also fun and love, as there is with brothers. "That's what we keep saying."[24]

Apparently Ringo was the fragile one, with John saying that of the four men John worried the most about how the Beatles breakup would affect Ringo. At first, it was rocky but it seems Ringo has become what today is a relatively stable love and peace-sign proponent. Ringo's attitude in his All-Starr Band (formed in 1989), a traveling roster of musicians famous in their own right, has been to park the egos at the door, be supportive and keep it light: "…we will do our best for each other."[25]

As a band, the Beatles had enormous success. But the lesson from the Beatles, according to "Get Back" documentary filmmaker Peter Jackson is how they reacted to challenges. This, Jackson says, revealed their personalities.[26]

"Okay, so what's the takeaway?" It's the next morning, and BSwan is poised over a pad of paper, pen in hand, forehead resting in the other hand. The three in the drone think for a moment, then begin firing off points. [27]

1. Keep your sense of humour, to stay loose, relaxed and creative.
2. Work out your ideas away from the group, then bring them in for feedback.
3. There will be disagreements. Acknowledge anyone who takes a leadership role that keeps group focus.
4. Take breaks. Encourage new ideas. Welcome outside contribution.
5. Keep true to your roots. What was the initial spark that brought you together?
6. Respect everyone's contribution.
7. Give everyone space to be themselves.
8. Observe group dynamics. How are things changing?

Before the next set of stories, WSpace, GArea and BSwan are ready to get off the drone, stretch their legs, and get some fresh air and exercise. After GArea's turn at the drone controls, they begin to slowly descend into a rose-tinted dawn.

* * *

REVIEW:

1. What quality did each member of the Beatles bring to the band? How did it help and/or hinder them getting along?
2. How did the Beatles as a band change from beginning to end? What have you learned from their story about getting along?
3. What were Beatles core values?

Explain your choice: a) making money b) creativity c) brotherhood, or?

CHAPTER TWO -
Culture Speaks

All life is circular, the changing seasons and life stages moving through to death then repeating again. The physical, emotional, mental and spiritual are intimately connected.

BACK TO THE BEGINNING

PREVIEW:

1. What do you know about Indigenous worldviews?
2. How are they different from non-Indigenous worldviews? Give an example.

* * *

"Your music kept me awake last night." "What?" "You heard me. Your music kept me awake last night." The drone is silently descending into a valley of deep green. The three grab something to eat, and sit at the table in their hiking boots, jackets, caps and scarves, a small backpack at the ready. GArea is annoyed at BSwan.

"But I was listening on my headphones," BSwan tells him quizzically, mouth agape, catching his eye. "It must have been really loud, 'cause I could hear it," GArea counters jaw clenched, shifting to face BSwan full on. "The walls of the pods are really thin." "I thought you liked that singer?"

GArea snorts, "Sure! But not at one in the morning, and not all night on repeat."

"Oh, I'm sorry! I must have fallen asleep." BSwan's voice is soft and low. "I'll turn it off at 11, okay? Will make it up to you."

"Ya, sure." GArea turns away, and watches bleary-eyed as the drone makes its descent.

The landing is smooth and the locking mechanism clicks open before the door slides to the left. WSpace, GArea and BSwan hoist their packs, WSpace leading the way out into the dappled sunshine of a forest clearing. The three walk in silence along a well-trodden trail, breathing in the cool air, the ancient trees massive, to one side somewhere the rush of a creek. It's beautiful, midday, the sun beating down. They climb a rise and sit looking out over the expanse in the distance, no road or civilization in sight. "Do you know where we are?" WSpace peers into the distance, cupping her eyes against the sun.

"No, haven't a clue," GArea says breathing heavily after the hill climb, and wiping his brow. "I don't think we're supposed to know. It's a pit stop."

"So beautiful," WSpace muses. "Such a different world. Nature as a church."

"The way the world was for a very long time," BSwan adds, foraging in a pack.

"I'm thinking of Indigenous Peoples," WSpace continues deep in thought, "and thousands of years of their own way to get along."

"Yep." GArea saunters behind a bush to urinate. "Differences in worldview."

GArea sits back down, and the three talk for some time about the basic way of life common to many Indigenous Peoples around the world. Awe and respect for all living and non-living things, inter-dependence, a bond that shapes their human relationships.

All life is circular, the changing seasons and life stages moving through to death then repeating again. The physical, emotional, mental and spiritual are intimately connected. WSpace talks of the sacred wheel common to many Indigenous cultures: stone, or otherwise in logos, drums and artwork with four quadrants, with perhaps a centre that represents learning, self, balance and beauty.[1]

GArea leans against a rock listening. WSpace talks of the importance of balance in all things, and how women in many Indigenous communities lead the way in teaching and promoting balance. BSwan lies on the ground, the sky gleaming off dark sunglasses. At one point, WSpace reminds BSwan of the Indigenous acceptance of non-binary gendered people, the two spirited.[2] BSwan swings one leg over the other, puts hands behind head and nods.

WSpace talks of how educating children in the family and community is wholistic and starts early, based on when individual kids are ready. Knowledge and skills are withheld until children can understand and appreciate the importance, which might be at different ages. Three sources of Indigenous knowledge are: one's own experience in the world, the passed-down oral experience of Elders, and - equally important - what comes to a person through dreams, the mystical spirit world.[3] BSwan sits up and crosses legs. "Ya, I really like that part. It opens a person's perspective to the unexpected, the unanticipated, which is part of life, too, right? Awesome."

WSpace nods her head, takes a drink of water, and wraps her arms around her bent knees. From a distance comes a familiar hum. A dot on the horizon grows larger then is recognizable as the drone. It's time for the next story.

* * *

REVIEW:

1. What role does the "circle" concept play in Indigenous worldviews? Explain.

2. How might the "circle" concept play a role in conflict transformation?

Can she trust others in this strange Old World? Can they trust her? It comes slowly, the respect and trust. But it comes.

CULTURE WARP

PREVIEW:

1. How do people build respect and trust? How do people destroy it?
2. Is forgiveness the same as reconciliation? Explain.

* * *

Building Respect and Trust

Twisting. Turning. Fog. Falling. Blinded. Then it was done. She lay panting. Forest. Numbing cold. Silence. But not for long. In Diana Gabaldon's novel series "Outlander," the character Claire Randall fell through time, from 1945 to 1743 Scotland. In the days, weeks and years to come, she was tested time and again. Could she trust others in this strange Old World? Could they trust her? It came slowly, the respect and trust. But it came.[1]

Claire was acutely sensitive to the actions and behavior of the people around her. The clothing, language, customs, and accepted interaction were unfamiliar and yet somehow comfortingly familiar. Adults played with youngsters in loving ways. Motherly women looked after their circle of family and community, while men chatted and laughed among each other.

Some customs appeared primitive, and made no sense to Claire, a wartime battle nurse, but she respected other customs that seemed effective and efficient. She learned that people in the past weren't less sophisticated, less wise, or less knowledgeable. Claire learned from her captors, and they learned from her.

In this new-to-her life, she had to read every gesture for nuance, and try to fit in as best she could. It was a collision of cultures - old and new. She had to use everything she knew from her past life in the 21st century to transform and translate into what was available to her immediately in the 18th century. Many of these men would die in battle at Culloden. Claire knew it was coming. Life for these proud Highlanders was hard. They were at the height of their culture, clansmen wearing kilts and speaking Gaelic, traditionally an oral storytelling culture. Most of them were farmers just trying to feed their families.[2]

Centuries earlier, the Romans had built Hadrian's Wall along this northwestern boundary of the Roman empire, to keep away these Celtic "barbarians."[3] For the Celtic Highlanders death lurked from everyday illness, but also from brutal conflict with the southerners, the despised English. This strange woman Claire healed their worst injuries without flinching. She was useful, observant, willing to learn, but still English.

Regardless, in Gabaldon's fictional world the Highlanders brought Claire into their social circle and married her off to one of their most handsome but least desirable men (as a social prospect). Jamie Fraser was a soldier wanted by the English military.[4]

Together, Jamie and Claire survived the battle at Culloden, and set their sights across the ocean for a new start in the "New World." Claire told Jamie the future of the American frontier and how its ancestral Indigenous Peoples would be overrun as were the Scottish Highlanders.[5]

Like the fictitious tale of the English nurse Claire but in reverse, settlers and Indigenous Peoples in North America look back in time to 1763 and English King George III's Royal Proclamation for a way forward. The Proclamation could have made for a more compassionate "nation-to-nation" relationship. It was relatively respectful based on an international understanding that Indigenous Peoples - the "inhabitants" - were the original owners of their land, and must be recognized as owners. However, by the time Canada became a country 100 years later, the inhabitants weren't treated as owners but underlings who had to fit somehow into English, Scottish and French society.[6]

Like Claire Randall, sometimes in life a person may feel they've been dropped in to another place and time where they don't belong. Inhabitants may not feel the person belongs either.

Forgiveness is a hard, weighty process of grieving. Forgiveness is not denying what has happened or forgetting, but finally putting the past in the past, putting down that load in order to move forward, and not necessarily together. (On the other hand, reconciliation involves building mutual trust and moving forward together.) [7]

Both forgiveness and reconciliation assume any bad behavior is left behind in the past. But what if the bad behavior continues? What then?

* * *

REVIEW:

1. What is the role of grieving before a person can forgive? Explain.
2. What is the significance of the Royal Proclamation's core values to Indigenous Peoples and settlers? Explain.
3. What does the Outlander story of Claire Randall have to do with relations between settlers and Indigenous Peoples? Explain.

Actions build reputation, for better or worse.

CROSSING OCEANS AND CROSSING PATHS

PREVIEW:
1. What does it mean to "make a name" for yourself? What does it have to do with getting along? Explain. To what extent does it mean the same as building a "reputation"?
2. If you are in a new country, what is important to get along? Explain.
3. What can be bad about trying to "fit in" to get along? Explain.

* * *

Do I Know You?
Respect and trust. We earn it by our actions. Actions build reputation, for better or worse. Reputation affects those around us from our family, friends and workplace to everyone else we meet. It can lead to tension, or help smooth the waters. The name we make for ourself through daily interactions can either soar like the sun, or sink like a stone.

Building Reputation Through Hope
For an immigrant, personal reputation is created from nothing, zero, the beginning. We start with the choice to leave home and everything familiar, with little in the pocket but hope, faith that life will be better, blessed ignorance, and maybe a small immigrant community to give moral support. We start with the energy to work hard and keep putting one foot in front of the other, the desire to fit in.

The reputation of ethnic background or country of origin (or stereotypes) may arrive before us for better or worse. What does past history say about *this* person's background, life experience, perspective, point of view? Are these impressions helping or hurting *this* new immigrant trying to make a name and build a reputation?

Not Just Another "Hole" in the Ground

The painting sat on the mantle of the woman's gas fireplace. In the painting, a tiny figure sits puffing on a pipe, on the top step of a long grass-roofed wooden building surrounded by tall snow-tipped mountains in the distance.

It was 1949. Her paternal grandfather Hans John Hole had returned after World War II for a visit to his mountain village in western Norway for the first time since he left 44 years prior when he was 16 years old and never saw his parents again.

She wondered at the thoughts going through his head. A mountain village boy followed some of his brothers across the ocean to a land where streets were said to be "paved with gold." His goal was a bicycle.

He changed his last name from Hole ("Hoo-le") to Henningson (grandson of Henning) to be more appropriate in English. In the following years, he followed the work from California farms northeast to the mines of Montana, north to Alaska, then back down the coast to settle in the Vancouver area, marry a quiet Swedish housemaid, have five children, and build a construction company.[1]

He experienced early unionism unfolding, and maintained a life-long empathy for the economic challenges of "the working man." The English and Scottish seemed to have privilege and advantage and got the good jobs. Scandinavians, on the other hand, were often low-wage manual labourers. Some tended toward feelings of inferiority. The message the Norwegian young man took from society was "be likable to get ahead in life."

Getting Along in Africa: "God Within" Quakers Meet Maragoli Pacifists

What's in a name? The surname "Hole" isn't limited to Norway. Take Kenya, for example. Here in Africa, a U.S. Midwest missionary named Edgar T. Hole among others had a big impact (apparently unrelated to our teenage Norwegian immigrant).

In 1902, three years prior to the Norwegian teenager's voyage, Edgar followed two other young Quaker missionaries named Willis R. Hotchkiss and Arthur B. Chilson from the U.S. to Kenya. ("Quaker" refers to the 1600s Christian movement in England that rejected "go-betweens" such as priests and ministers. Instead, Quakers believe God is in everyone, and value peacebuilding). Though it was Willis' idea to go to Africa he didn't stay long, leaving it to Arthur, Edgar and early Kenyan Quakers to gather new

Christians, and also help Kenyans develop income and vocational training. They built houses, roads and a sawmill with dam on the 1,000-acre plot given them by British occupiers, later followed by an agricultural school, teacher-training school, and technological institute. Kenyan traditional oral stories were turned into written language.[2]

What made Quakerism successful in Kenya with the Maragoli (Mulembe) people was the common value of peace. It fit with their native spirituality, including shamanic healing practice called "Umwahi." They saw themselves reflected in each other. It was a cultural connection that helped the two to get along. Fourth generation Kenyan Quaker Stanley Chagala Ngesa (an initiated Maragoli shaman who holds a MDiv degree from San Francisco Theological Seminary) says he's "fascinated" by how Quaker and Maragoli culture combined "without one erasing the other." Maragoli means "peace," and Maragoli have always been pacifist, practicing agriculture in western Kenya for centuries (near the equator at Lake Victoria, the second largest freshwater lake in the world). They originally came upstream from Misri, Egypt, along the Nile River.[3]

There are also common links between the Maragoli and Indigenous Peoples elsewhere in Australia and North America. Maragoli elders pass on their oral traditions through different rites of passage for boys and girls, boys spending time in the "initiation forest." Maragoli people share dreams through a nightly bonfire circle with talking stick. This circle is key to community life and expression of hopes for the future. Listening is highly valued along with the speaking. (Australian aborigines call a similar meditative circle-based dream check-in "pinakarri.") According to Chagala Ngesa, dreams are the way gods and ancestors - which include all aspects of nature - speak to the Maragoli. Everything in nature has a living soul.[4]

Kenyans are conservative Quakers who see "God within" as basically Jesus Christ. Unlike the Western Liberal wing of the movement who meet for silent worship, the Kenyans are more comfortable as "noisy Quakers," said Pastor Simon Khaemba of the Friends International Service in Nairobi, with a worship service that features music, choral singing, closed eyes and raised hands.[5]

As of 2017, there were approximately 400,000 Quakers around the world in 87 countries. Kenya led the way with 119,285 (compared to the

United States 80,092, Burundi 47,600, Bolivia 28,500, United Kingdom 23,067, Guatemala 19,830 and Canada 1,300).[6]

Since World War II, Kenyan Quakers have taken on more official leadership. Quaker schools have been government-run as of Kenyan independence in 1963. (There are more than 1,500 Quaker primary schools, high schools and colleges, two hospitals and hundreds of clinics and dispensaries.) In 1986, Friends Church Kenya was formed to coordinate 20 Quaker groups ("yearly meetings") and peace education. African Quakers are active in peacemaking efforts in Uganda, Tanzania, Rwanda and Burundi. Quakerism has also spread to the south, central and some northern areas of Africa.[7]

Wartime Disrespect

Despite the common Quaker value of peace, wartime experience in Kenya under British occupation brought hardship for the Maragoli. Kenyans were conscripted by the British occupiers to fight in World War I (1914-19), and many never returned, their records lost forever. According to Chagala Ngesa, the British colonizers didn't see the Kenyans as "fully human."[8]

Like some North American Indigenous Peoples during the residential school period, the Kenyans realized they needed to learn the ways of the West in order to begin to make a place for themselves "as teachers, local officials, medical workers, farmers and businesspeople."[9]

Maragoli Point of View

Native worldview continues to guide the Maragoli today, Khaemba said, and they take "an African perspective." Kenyan Quakers stay positive and constructive, Chagala Ngesa said, particularly regarding the dominant western culture which tends to justify "war and waste and glorifies selfish behavior." Dominant world religions have much to learn from native peoples' faith traditions. Shamanic teaching, for example, is that "no one can crush a person," said Chagala Ngesa's great-grandmother Dorika. Though her husband disappeared in World War I, to her his spirit lived "right here, where we are." [10]

* * *

PART ONE - FAMOUS OR UNSUNG

WSpace, GArea, and BSwan sit in Quaker-style silence, their heads bowed. The tiny clock in the kitchenette marks the seconds. One minute. Two. BSwan's head begins to nod, then a gentle snore.

At five minutes, WSpace brings them back. "Who would like to be our recording clerk?" GArea and BSwan look at each other, GArea staring down BSwan. "I guess I could do it," BSwan murmurs, pushing locks of hair from eyes, reaching for a pen and paper, and writing a title heading. "Great. Share inspiration as it comes to you," WSpace says. "Leave a short space of silence between what each person says. Remember, 'God in everyone,' so each person's comment has worth to be considered equally and deeply." The three settle in to their chairs. Silence. Then GArea starts.

"That whole thing about surname, what's in a name? making a name? It's got me thinking. We're born with our name. We go through life with it. What were our ancestors like before us with that name? The rest of the family. The Maragoli pride in their heritage. People judge us just by our name, lump us into a category. Out of our control." Silence.

"Ya, but the Norwegian kid changed it, just like that," BSwan snaps fingers. "Took control of what people might think." Silence.

"'A rose by any other name would smell as sweet,' WSpace pipes up, quoting Shakespeare.[11] "The Norwegian kid is still the same person regardless of name. Then there's 'making a name' for yourself. That's all about reputation. That's totally the person being in control." Silence.

"Kind of, having a good or bad 'rep'," BSwan leans forward, really getting into it. "Different from getting a 'bad rap,' which means being criticized, right?" Silence.

More silence. "We don't talk about 'reputation' much," GArea starts thoughtfully. "Sometimes it's linked in with ego and being self-centred. You know, 'it might tarnish my reputation' so I don't take action. Fear of social rejection." The other two nod. Silence.

"But that's what life's all about, isn't it?" WSpace's face is turned to one side. "The reputation we build everyday from our actions. People around us are bound to judge, one way or the other." Silence.

"Right. Folks start to see us as this kind of person, or that kind." BSwan is nodding. "Sometimes we think it's kind of easier to just leave and start again somewhere else. Hmm." Silence. "That may not be true."

Over the next hour, they turn their attention to the connection forged between Quakers and Marigoli Kenyans. It has been complicated, no doubt, due to occupation by foreigners but it shows how a relationship can be built and nurtured based on recognized core values, as long as each side really observes and pays attention to the other.

Things change. The Quaker experiment in Kenya shows the power in numbers, with an overwhelming modern-day population embracing "noisy" conservative Quakerism, reminiscent of evangelical Christianity. On the other hand, population numbers can be counterbalanced by a power due to prosperity. Liberal Quakers tend to be older and practice the original silent meetings for worship. They also tend to have more funds.

What does it say about getting along? Dealing with conflict? It's easy to feel threatened by the other's power in numbers or prosperity. It's more difficult to be calm, relax, and focus on what can be learned and shared.

* * *

REVIEW:

1. Why is Stanley Chagala Ngesa "fascinated" by how Quakers and Kenyan Maragoli get along together in Kenyan society?

2. This chapter includes both positive and negative ways British occupiers and Kenyans co-existed together. What are they?

3. What core values do Quakers and Kenyan Maragoli have in common? Explain your choices.

"For the little girl, learning to read and write at school meant friends and social connection. But for Grandfather Tematargay education divided a community between the educated and the uneducated. There was judgment of what was superior and inferior."

HIMALAYAN WOMEN MAKING IT WORK

PREVIEW:

1. How does education both help and hinder a community to get along?
2. What is the role of expectations in a group when it comes to getting along?

* * *

From "Marianne" to "Angmo"

As WSpace, GArea and BSwan prepare to increase their oxygen intake, the drone rises up over the densely populated African continent, veering east over the Arabian Sea. The drone soars higher and higher as it nears northern India then the high altitudes of Nepal and the Himalayas with their relatively sparse pockets of few and tiny family villages dotting the valleys.

Some archeologists say pre-historic human migration moved in an Eastern direction from Africa to the Middle East, Asia then across a land bridge to North America.[1] In the 1990s, 29-year-old ethnologist and award-winning filmmaker Marianne Chaud crouched silently on her haunches with a Himalayan grandmother and children, staring out over the silent deep narrow valley, and peaks of the Himalayas, the highest mountain range in the world.[2]

The villagers gave her the Zanskar name "Angmo," welcomed her into their homes, and accepted her as a foreign daughter and sister. On her part, she learned their language. Over seven years, she returned annually to spend a few months with four generations of the mountain women and girls as they harvested barley (their one viable food crop at this altitude) and prepared for winter. Each trip into the high valley meant a four-day trek.[3]

"Sking" is one of the most isolated villages in the Zanskar region of northern India, at 13,000 feet in altitude. The women of all ages are mainly the ones to harvest the crops from sun up to sun down August through October while the men help store the harvest. Over the years, Angmo spent time in various villages, interested, studious, listening, and also expected to work along with the women.[4]

Her video camera recorded their life. The first day looking curiously in the camera viewfinder, Grandmother Kunzes was pleased to see she still had teeth, feeling the front of her mouth.

Her 30-something daughter Katup, mother to two little girls and a baby boy, matter-of-factly told Angmo of their wedding traditions. In her own case, during a visit to an aunt in a neighbouring village, Katup was kidnapped by six strong young men sent by her future husband Norbu. Katup and Norbu were married the next day, their first child born nine months later. Katup valued Norbu as a good husband.[5]

Grandmother Kunzes' husband Tematargay dismissed with a scoff mention of the other village Angmo stayed in the previous year. (He worked odd jobs outside the village as muleteer, carpenter or painter.) According to Tematargay, Sking is a better, calmer community because no one has studied and become arrogant. Sking people are equal.

No one has studied, but 13-year-old shepherd girl Sapel previously attended Grade 1. Otherwise Sapel had herded the village sheep since she was seven in return for extra food for her family. It was hard work, boring and lonely, she said with a smile, and school would be nice.

A jet plane overhead was an object of fascination to the young village girls. Sapel asked Angmo what the cost was to take a trip in a plane. Another girl named Isephel wondered how many rugs were in the plane for seating. Maybe 150 chairs but no rugs, Angmo said, leaving Isephel to contemplate such an idea.

Eighty-year-old great-grandmother Rickzine asked Angmo if Rickzine's granddaughter wanted Rickzine to finish cutting the barley in the field. Rickzine had been blind the previous four years, and was feeling the heat of the sun as she sat on the ground, shaving the barley close to the roots with her short cutting sickle. She and Angmo talked of the shortness of life, of Rickzine's age. Rickzine was tired, and decided to nap where she sat, her face uplifted to the sun, before going back to the family dwelling for dinner. She would die three days later.

As Chaud narrates, Buddhist non-attachment is key for the Zanskar villagers, who have a favorite saying that all life is constant change.[6] But the family mourned Rickzine. As well, when it was time for Angmo to leave the valley, Katup the young mother was sad. She regretted her own isolated life. In an effort to comfort Katup, Angmo pointed to the challenging trek ahead, and said Katup was the lucky one to be safe at home.

In March 2000, on the release of her documentary "Himalaya: Land of Women", Marianne Chaud ("Angmo") said that becoming attached to the Sking women helps the outside world to know itself better. However, she predicted the village isolation was in peril. Chaud foresaw a drivable road in 10 years that would cross the region north to south bringing goods, army trucks and tourist buses all year.[7]

In 2023, an online travel guide touted the Zanskar region's monasteries, palace, waterfall and lake. It told of shared cabs especially in August and September when the roads are still open before winter (traveling more than 10-12 hours to get to key Zanskar landmarks with one break, but four or five toilet stops).[8]

* * *

"Okay, there's that thing about names again," BSwan is staring intently out the drone cockpit, as the Sking village scene recedes in the distance. WSpace and GArea turn back to the table and each other for comment. "Like, what these villagers are doing is giving Marianne Chaud a name from their culture that has meaning already built into it. No reputation-building needed. The villagers are showing high regard for her, showing acceptance, connection, inclusion. and respect."

"Good point, Swan," WSpace murmurs. "What does 'Angmo' mean, anyway?"

BSwan swings around for a phone, and begins searching the internet. "Got it! Found something with meanings submitted by users." [9] BSwan straightens, clears the throat, and begins with authority. "Okay, it's mostly a Tibetan name, but also used in Indian Sanskrit, and Hindi. Yah, right on. Um... seems to be generally a girl's name. Means very confident, assertive, gets angry easily." GArea guffaws slightly. BSwan glares reproachfully at him, and continues. "Stubborn, intelligent. The Tibetan meaning can be something like 'Queen.'" GArea laughs outright. BSwan stops and turns to GArea in exasperation.

"Well, that's a bit ironic, don't you think," GArea says, "for a foreigner sauntering into their quiet mountain valley?" WSpace is rolling her eyes. "Yes, it's a great documentary, and think about it!" GArea continues. "Reverse the roles. What if instead, a Zanskar villager waltzed into a modern city and announced that the Zanskari person was there to go everywhere, watch and record! Haha! I mean, the gall. It's kind of taking advantage of vulnerability and lack of sophistication in modern ways."

WSpace and BSwan agree that ethnologists and Western explorers have historically made a habit of going "where no man has gone before," welcome or not.

But WSpace has heard enough. "Chaud appears to be sensitive to that. She's recording the process of change in the valley, and building relationships. Making the effort to learn the language is huge."

"For as long as she's there which isn't really for that long," GArea breaks in.

Talk turns to the role of language: the Norwegian teenager, Kenyan Maragoli pacifists, and now Himalayan villagers. One thing the drone team agrees on is that language is the core of a culture, a group of people, a circle of belonging. It's the heart and soul. One of the quickest ways to show someone they belong is to share your language as the Sking villagers did with Marianne Chaud.

BSwan has a sudden thought. "But we're not necessarily talking literacy here when we talk about language, are we?" GArea pounces on the opening. "Very good point, Swan. For the little girl, learning to read and write at school meant friends and social connection. But for Grandfather Tematargay education divided a community between the educated and the uneducated. There was judgment of what was superior and inferior. Things weren't level anymore. People had a harder time to understand each other. It threatened the way they did things in the valley!"

PART ONE - FAMOUS OR UNSUNG

"As for Katup being kidnapped by friends of her future husband Norbu," GArea isn't done yet, "I'm thinking that the villagers gave Marianne Chaud the name 'Angmo' for a reason. They didn't see foreign women like her very often traipsing around the high Himalaya."

"And neither do the rest of us, for that matter," WSpace laughs gently.

"We don't know the details," GArea continues, "such as whether Katup and Norbu were engaged before the 'kidnapping,' which would have made it more of a kind of ceremonial ritual.

"But we get the impression that, though the women work hard in the fields, traditions in their society can have them quite passive. Okay, I'm done. So, Swan, what's for dinner?"

The drone shudders during its slow descent to the east from the silence of the high Himalaya. BSwan walks to the fridge, then falls heavily against a wall, as the drone takes a steep sudden lurch to the left and picks up speed, wind screaming through its outer wings.

"Turbulence!" GArea yells. WSpace topples onto the floor from her chair, struggles to grab hold, and drags herself around the table.

"Get to the pods!" she gasps. The three crawl to one side desperately using chairs as leverage, sending dishes crashing, and skidding to one corner.

"No!" she screams, "not at the same time!"

Too late, the drone flips, and everything including GArea, BSwan, and WSpace hurtle up to the ceiling, Swan bashing an arm "oooww!"

The drone is speeding through the lower Himalaya, its auto-pilot sending it weaving in and out of high valleys, tossing WSpace, GArea and BSwan from one side of the open work area to the other. The drone gradually rights itself, gains some balance, and they hear the mechanism start once again.

WSpace moans. "Oh my god..." BSwan is on the floor next to the fridge, bowed and cradling an arm. GArea has a nasty cut to one side of his left eye, and lies sprawled on his back. WSpace is covered in a heap of furniture, paper and cutlery, bruised but still able to move.

Nothing breaks the silence, except for their breathing, and a dripping tap. "Oh my god," she repeats, her eyes wide and jaw open. "What was that?"

GArea hoists himself to one side, and slowly mouths the words. "We've got to get ready for our next two stories!" he gasps. "The Mongol Queens, then it's the last of the Chinese matriarchy cultures!"

* * *

REVIEW:

1. What role does language play in the relationship between ethnologist Marianne Chaud and the Zanskar villagers? Chaud is not a blood relative to the villagers. Why do they call her their foreign daughter and sister?

2. Chaud said that becoming attached to the Sking women helps the outside world to know itself better. What does Chaud mean?

If it's 1206 and you're a 16-year-old daughter of Genghis Khan the "Great Khan," you've been groomed to take power, and rule. You and the women of your family played a major role to manage the largest empire the world has ever known.

MONGOL QUEENS

PREVIEW:

1. How do you rule an empire effectively? Explain.
2. How can a person be successful as an "underdog"? Explain.

* * *

The drone had restored itself. Dry sandy hills along the flat winding ribbon of Yellow River curled ahead to the northeast as far as the eye could see, the midday sun glinting off the muddy water far below.

For much of the first half of the last millennium, this was a major international crossroads, with a cosmopolitan melding of cultures and people from across the continent and beyond: Mediterranean, Indian, Muslim, Chinese. A typical neighbourhood market today in Gansu province gives a sense: skewers of lamb in cumin barbecued over high flames at streetside stalls, raw meat hanging from hooks, piles of fresh fruits and vegetables, and rows of large baskets across the floor filled to the brim with nuts, dried fruit, spices.

This was the Silk Route, funneling Western roads through Gansu "like water through a canyon." Merchants came together over the 1,000-mile corridor, their destination the ancient Chinese city of Xian to the east.[1]

In the shadow of this bustling world market, out of the northwest high steppes the Mongolian conqueror Genghis Khan rode with 100,000 soldiers – vastly outnumbered - across the formidable barrier of the Gobi Desert.

Flash forward. It's the 20st century. You're 16 years old. What are your options? If it's 1905, and you're a Norwegian farm boy from the mountains dreaming of buying a bicycle, you might cross an ocean by steamship to look for work on another continent. A young Quaker missionary from the

U.S. Midwest of the same generation might do the same. If it's the late 1950's and you're a motherless high school student with dreams of making money and becoming famous, you might form a rock band.

But if it was 1206 and you were a 16-year-old daughter of Genghis Khan the "Great Khan," you were groomed to take power, and rule. You were expected to marry strategically to create an alliance between tribes, and, when necessary, lead your thousands of mounted soldiers into battle. You and the women of your family played a major role to manage the largest empire the world has ever known. Alaqai Beki, at 16 or 17 years old, was the first of Genghis Khan's nomadic family from the Mongolian Plateau to ride out from a pastoral world to conquer the urban world of China, what anthropologist and historian Jack Weatherford calls "one of the greatest conquests in Asian history." The Chinese loathed and feared the Mongolians, who they saw as unsettled brutes. Alaqai Beki's eventual multicultural kingdom covered a large part of what is now Chinese Inner Mongolia. How to get along as a conqueror's daughter? The Great Khan's advice to Alaqai Beki was to ride in stride with him, and match his every move. She must keep herself safe at all cost, trust her own judgement, make ongoing learning a major priority, and be "prudent, steadfast, and courageous." She wasn't just the one in power, he said. She was the one responsible for those she ruled. She needed to keep focused on how history would remember her.[2]

Genghis Khan made the conquests. But it was his daughters, not his less capable sons, who turned the conquests into "the world's first truly international empire" from the Pacific to the Mediterranean with trade, education, religious tolerance, and an economic system. Stories of these warrior horsewomen shocked Europe and the Islamic world.[3]

After Genghis Khan's death in 1227, the Mongol queens lost power as daughters and daughters-in-law squabbled, and brothers and sons challenged their leadership.

It would be 243 years later before power would again pass to a woman, Queen Manduhai, a young widow without connections but wily and strong-willed (whose name means the rising of the sun). Manduhai restored order by personally leading her horsemen in multiple victories, and ruled for 39 years from 1470 to 1509, an outstanding legacy. In her 30s she married a

17-year-old prince (orphan Dayan Khan), the only living male descendent of Genghis Khan. They had eight children in a career she spent fighting the Ming Dynasty of China on one side and a series of Muslim warlords on the other – even while pregnant. Her success reinforced the Chinese commitment to northern defensive walls.[4]

* * *

BSwan's right arm is in a sling. There's a bandage at GArea's left eye. WSpace has an aching large blue bump on her forehead. Her right eye is black as if she'd been punched. The three look dazed, gawking out the drone window, loose-jawed, slumped in their chairs.

"I've read Weatherford's book." GArea and BSwan swing to stare at WSpace. "When'd you have time to do that?" GArea asks incredulous. "You've been running on the treadmill."

"It's great stuff," she enthuses. "We were talking about the role of a name, and making a name for oneself. Genghis Khan was one charismatic guy, and he knew how to organize people. The Mongolians set things up according to name and number, so Genghis Khan organized his empire that way. They used even not odd numbers for practical stuff. More spiritual stuff had odd numbers. His father's name 'Yesugei' meant 'with nines'. It carried a lot of good fortune, because it meant you were at the centre of life's eight directions and would never get lost." A smile is playing on GArea's lips. WSpace pats her bruised eye gently, and shifts further back in her chair. "Like many Mongols, Genghis Khan's name came from his parent, so he was 'son of nines,' and he took that name really seriously." WSpace is becoming more and more animated, her eyes sparkling. "Genghis Khan planned everything so he'd be in the number nine spot. He started out with a personal guard of 800 by day and 800 by night, then switched it to 10,000 guards, the ninth unit after his eight-unit army."[5] GArea and BSwan's mouths are open, eyes wide.

"And the women?" GArea rouses himself to ask.

"The eight kids with the most potential shared power and responsibility: four sons as 'khans' and four daughters as queens. Genghis Khan figured he needed a few rulers and centres of power, so he gave the sons the nomadic steppes, a bunch of hard-drinking partiers, and not too effective. He gave the daughters the kingdoms that stayed put, along the Silk Route from northern China through Central Asia, and these gals were much more effective."

WSpace leans forward pointedly. "Genghis Khan ruled over it all. As Weatherford says, '[never] before or since have women exercised so much power over so many people and ruled so much territory for as long as these women did.'"[6]

"Awesome." BSwan murmurs, fascinated.

"Okay, so the number of sons and daughters in power were the same," GArea says.

"Yes, but there's more. Genghis Khan wanted to better his dad, so he aimed for the magic number 13 instead of nine, and organized the empire into 13 camps. The first circle had his four dowager queens (his wives) in control. The outer circle was those sons and daughters."[7]

Early on, the daughters, especially the senior queen, Alaqai Beki, got very involved in setting up a working government. She was the highest-ranking Mongol south of the Gobi, and ruled the largest part of the empire (apart from her father). Alaqai Beki learned to read and write, studied medicine, set up medical facilities, and apparently was influential in educating the Muslim world and the West about Chinese medicine. She took the best from the various cultures, and tolerated the various religions. The daughters judged criminal cases, and wrestled men in public contests. Some of these daughters accepted arranged husbands. Others chose other men, or none at all. Some had kids. Others didn't.[8]

"The people they conquered didn't necessarily welcome these women with open arms," WSpace stresses. "The local people may have been a bit impressed but, to them these daughters were a bit strange. They didn't behave like local women. They didn't bind their feet, for example. Some of the local people thought the Mongol queens were immoral, against the local religion, even a threat to society." WSpace adds that almost as soon as Genghis Khan died the family started tearing down the power of the women rulers, and the empire suffered for it.[9]

"Amazing," BSwan murmurs softly. "Like, how did these folks get to be so powerful? Wouldn't call it 'getting along' as such, because they were conquerors. But they had to be getting along with someone to make it all work."

PART ONE - FAMOUS OR UNSUNG

The Great Khan married off his daughters and granddaughters to surrounding tribal leaders and their sons to increase influence, WSpace says, to gain and sustain power, by building connections, networks, alliances. By doing so, he took full advantage of his few resources (his family). Every move was strategic, with Genghis Khan instructing the women that their job was to rule, to organize and control. There would be no co-ruler. He told his daughter Checheyigen to always show wisdom and sincerity. The son-in-law, on the other hand, was removed from the scene, to join the Mongol army and fight with Genghis Khan. The Great Khan showed no mercy to those who opposed him, WSpace continues. At the same time, he was visionary and persistent in trying different approaches (such as how to move his forces back and forth across the Gobi Desert). At the beginning, he'd make allies with tribes who would serve as waystations for his then relatively small army of 100,000 soldiers if they needed somewhere to retreat to.[10]

"Genghis Khan's wife Borte also played a big part in the daughters' success," WSpace pulls her knees up to her chest, and wraps her arms around. "Borte raised their kids herself and taught them her tribe's values. The daughters were to be beautiful and clever, marry powerful men, and look after their home tribe. The daughters needed to have strong skills in negotiation and mediation." [11]

Thirteenth century Mongols weren't much for showing emotion. They honoured the fluids of a mother's body: blood in the womb, milk after birth, saliva that moistened the food she chewed for the growing child, urine to wash and sterilize wounds. But tears were dangerous. When it was time for sons and daughters to ride away to join the Great Khan's expeditions, these offspring were not to look back but "stare straight ahead into the future." As a Mongolian mother of that time, Borte would have held back her tears, walked far away from her family and "ger" (yurt tent), lain face down and cried her pain into the earth.[12]

WSpace looks down suddenly quiet, contemplative, thinking of her own daughter far away. BSwan and GArea holding steaming mugs of tea are feeling much better.

"So, with the Mongol queens of the 13th to 16th century, we're talking about human potential," GArea says. "Even if you start off being an underdog like Genghis Khan, there's a lot you can do if you work with what you have and get creative. Building alliances, for example."

"Ya, for sure," BSwan is nodding. "Sounds like Genghis Khan zeroed in on his empire's strengths, and that included the women. He didn't micromanage but delegated and let people do their work. He trusted them. And to do that he must have trained them pretty well. He had a system that worked.

"And you know, I'm thinking of the kind of risk Genghis Khan took at the beginning," BSwan continues. "It sort of took a lot of courage and belief in yourself."

WSpace nods then sighs. "They could be fantastic administrators, no doubt about that. But it was still a lot of 'power-over', violence, war. The one with the biggest stick won."

Together they hobble to the kitchen. With BSwan giving directions, before long the three are digging into a large plate of steamed dumplings, meat pies, boiled mutton, cheese and salted milk tea.[13]

* * *

REVIEW:

1. How did Mongol queen Alaqai Beki help create a successful kingdom? Explain.

2. How well did the Mongol queens fit in with the people they conquered? Explain.

3. What was Genghis Khan's core value: family, territory, money, being effective, names/numbers, or? Explain your choice.

She was next in line to take on a key leadership role. The pressure was intense, but it was her decision to make. What would she do? At least by Western standards, her family was no ordinary family.

CHINA'S LAST MATRIARCHY

PREVIEW:

1. Have you ever felt pressured by others to fit in with a group? Explain.
2. What does "family" mean to you? Explain.

* * *

The drone headed due south to Sichuan and Yunnan province, moving through the centuries to modern times. Skirting the Qinghai Tibetan Plateau to the west, it made its descent then hovered over a village hours away from any city, and one teenage girl in dark jeans and jacket as she went about her day.

Like many eighteen-year-olds around the world, Naka Matsu of Lijazui village was tormented with one decision haunting her day and night: this next year what life path would she choose? Documentary filmmaker Mathieu Schwartz followed Naka as the teenager considered her decision. At least for the next couple of years, Naka wanted to be a traditional cultural dancer in a dance troupe performing for tourists at Lugu Lake two hours by road from her isolated, rural home. But her family wanted her to stay to help run the household. She was next in line to take on a key leadership role. The pressure was intense, but it was her decision to make. What would she do? At least by Western standards, her family was no ordinary family.

Naka was born into a female-lead home (her grandmother's), as are most every child in the village. There was no father figure. And her mother's night partner of 25 years (Naka's father) was not her husband. (She didn't have a husband.) During the day, he lived in his mother's household, and helped support the children of his sisters and female cousins. What? Why? [1]

This is the last of western China's "kingdom of women." For centuries it was approximately 80 tribal alliances of 40,000 citizens and 10,000 soldiers, ruled by women. Through an adaptation of Buddhism, tribes worship not a god but a goddess.[2]

Today, the Mosuo ethnic group number around 40,000, and is still very much matrilineal in which a child is born into the mother's family. This is a curiosity to the outside world and a popular tourist draw for Chinese people themselves from elsewhere in the country. What is it that attracts them? They come to experience a family system that doesn't split couples from the maternal extended family. Instead, the extended family is the core of self-sufficient agriculture and animal husbandry, as well as child and elder care. According to Naka's great-uncle Nakajiaya a couple living on their own can't do everything.[3]

For the Mosuo, there is strength in the larger family group. They also respect sexual freedom for both men and women, a "walking marriage" by invitation of the woman, discretely at night in the woman's own "flowering" bedroom. There are no holding hands or kissing in public, Naka's mother Dasha Zuma said of her night relationship. There're no arguments. If a couple does end night visits, the extended family raises any children involved. There's a stable long-term commitment and affection, without disputes over child custody.[4] If a young person falls in love with one person and is faithful to that one person for a lifetime, great (and many do and are). If they prefer many sexual partners throughout their life, that's fine, too (which some do). There's no moral judgment. The Na language itself has no equivalent word for "jealousy." [5]

Lamu, the daughter of Naka's neighbour, married a man from outside the village, and runs a tourist restaurant two hours away with her husband. According to Lamu, the Mosuo attitude to sexual relations makes sense. It separates sexual relations from family and reproduction. According to Lamu, a woman's love life is her own private decision.[6] How does the Mosuo way of life work?

According to one source, children come of age early in their teens. A girl is given her own bedroom and the right to have sexual relations there, but only at night. If she gets pregnant her household (including brothers and uncles) help raise the child. Regardless of whether it's a girl or boy, the child takes on the maternal family name, and maternal property rights. However, according to Latami Dashi, Vice President of the Mosuo Culture Center, there is more involved in choosing a lover. It's a structured process. He says the accepted age for a visiting marriage is 21. The girl may spend three years watching the boy: how he gets along with others, treats elders, and helps out in the village. Parents must give their consent.[7]

Regardless, the biological father can take a more active role during the day with the maternal family with tasks or by bringing gifts but it's not required or expected. Who is the father? Sometimes it's not clear which may be a bit embarrassing, researcher Tami Blumenfield said, but not the social "no no" it is in some other cultures.[8]

The system has worked for the Mosuo for centuries. The matriarch is very powerful. She manages income, and decides each person's money and job. When it's time to pass leadership to a younger woman, the matriarch symbolically gives her the keys to the household storage.[9]

It doesn't mean that both men and women don't play a role in decision-making. Often, they're encouraged to give their opinion. Naka's uncle Dudji didn't want her to leave to join the dance troupe, because he said he couldn't afford to hire someone to replace her. But he did convince the family to build a guest house to attract tourists, by telling his family they would make more money from that patch of land than they could through agriculture.[10]

Women inherit the property. They focus on crops (plus grains, potatoes) and herds (yak, water buffalo, sheep, goats, poultry), while men do construction work, and are in charge of fishing and slaughtering livestock. A thriving Mosuo household may have a dozen salted or smoked whole pigs in storage that last for up to 10 years.[11]

Interestingly, Mosuo men deal with all things related to death, whether it be slaughtering pigs, warfare, or arranging a funeral (complete with cooking for guests). In modern times, Mosuo men have some political and religious power, which may not always have been the case.[12]

This is the way the Mosuo people do things, and it makes sense to them. Over the years, trade and political upset from outside didn't shake it. But modern technology and transportation are creating change. Young people such as Naka see what life is like on the outside, and some are leaving to find work elsewhere. Some are choosing to marry.

Naka's cousin Dawa was first in line to be the next matriarch. But she chose instead to marry a Chinese man, live in town, and have a child. At the time, the couple were laughed at, she said, adding that nowadays people in general are more open-minded. At times she missed the tight atmosphere of the extended family, and the help. (To keep peace, every child is treated the same.) In town, she looked after her daughter alone. The couple life, she said, can make the wife and husband self-centred. In contrast, Naka's friend Duma left the village, but came back to take over as matriarch of her own family, and carried on a long-distance relationship with the outside father of her young son. She did miss day-to-day life with her husband, she admitted, but it was always a joy when they got together.[13]

Nowadays, even some of the older men are looking for an income of their own outside the family. The older generation are anxious this will create problems with property and child/elder care in years to come. Also, their Daba priests (shamans) are aging. They're the keepers of cultural knowledge. How will the old ways be passed down to the next generation?[14]

Meanwhile, Naka made her decision and informed her family that she was leaving. In the days to follow, she prepared both herself and the villagers. The day of her departure, she packed her suitcase and hauled it out to the roadway. Her great uncle Nakajiaya sat smoking in the courtyard of the household compound. Though all may have felt emotional, there was little outward expression. Like the Mongols, there's no kisses, hugs or tears. The Mosuo focus on the joy of future homecoming.

Examples of other matrilineal societies in the world include among others: Sumatra, Indonesia (Minangkabau people, 8 million); Costa Rica and Panama (BriBri people, approximately 35,000); Sanburu, northern Kenya (Umoja refuge as of 1990); Ghana (Akan people, 20 million); Indian state of Meghalaya (Garo people); New Guinea (Nagovisi people); Northeastern Arizona (Hopi people, 19,000); Papua New Guinea (Trobrianders people); India (Khasi people) [15]

* * *

He is laughing uproariously, though the three in the drone can't quite see the humour.

"Ah, I can't believe it! Women in charge - sorry, WSpace." He pauses to get his breath. "No husbands. Hasn't worked very well for us here in the West, has it? A bunch of mixed-up kids, for what I can see."

WSpace smiles steely at Power Over, their team lead, via a video conference update on the drone threesome's progress. "There's more to it than that," She points out quietly.

"Oh right, there always is," he continues, his voice rising to a high waver. "'I'm so misunderstood.' So how's it going, anyway? Almost through with the stories? We've got a tight deadline, remember. '10 Steps to Getting Along: The Definitive Guide.' Should be a blockbuster!"

"Swan, how's the arm doing?" "Oh, better, better." BSwan sits up straighter. "Good! Glad to hear it."

"Gray, that eye still looks nasty. Should we schedule you for a check?" "Naw, naw, I'm fine. The antiseptic is doing its work." "Alright then, I'll let you get back to this matriarchy thing. Talk soon. Get 'er done, you three! The world is counting on you."

Then with a wave he's up out of his chair, and the screen goes black.

WSpace, GArea and BSwan release a collective sigh of relief, GArea rolling his eyes at WSpace. "Okay, that's over with. Let's get back to work."

WSpace's jaw is rigid and shoulders tight, her breathing shallow, as she stares at her notes. The room is quiet, except for the steady hum of the drone. BSwan coughs, then speaks haltingly.

"You know, I'm thinking what makes a matriarchy, kind of, is the religion. Is the god male or female?" BSwan is now waving one hand for emphasis. "And how does that happen? Going back centuries, there's probably a reason sort of but we don't know it. Ya, and maybe they don't know it either. So it wasn't you know predicted, anticipated. It just is. No one in their community made it happen, like, so no one has any more control over the situation than anyone else."

GArea nods, picks up a pen and twirls it. "Everyone in the community - including the biggest, brawniest macho male - has been brought up with the same value, that all life comes from a female source. You respect women - all women to the max." [16]

WSpace suddenly straightens. "Alright, so key to getting along for the Mosuo are shared values and expectations for how they interact, learned from childhood. That can change from culture to culture. What else?"

Over the next hour, the three - lead by WSpace - pin down key aspects of the Mosuo.

"Like, it's not easy," BSwan says, "to be torn between the modern world and your traditions. It's very disruptive to a family and how they talk together. You know, the Himalayan grandfather said it, too."

"Following the old way is relatively simple, in that sense," GArea adds. "Everyone knows the script."

"But we also have bright spots," WSpace smiles for the first time. "Uncle Dudji succeeds in convincing the family to build the guest house and make more money. He must have felt really good about that."

"If more tourism will help things in the long run," GArea points out. "The whole Mosuo thing really makes me more aware of how anyone is locked in to a culture. The father spends his time and energy with his *sister's* kids? Wow!"

"Ya, and Mosuo women say how annoying it is that tourists are always kind of asking about the sex," BSwan laughs. "as if it's a different person every night, which mostly doesn't seem to be the case. Human sex drive is accepted you know but the Mosuo idea of love still comes with boundaries and discretion: no holding hands or kissing in public, say."

GArea laughs. "A teenager gets pregnant? No problem! The family raises it. Must keep the population up, I'd think."

BSwan laughs with him, leaning forward. "Oh my god, but the young people also point out that, while their ritual dances are to connect kind of with the opposite sex, there aren't many sparks when you've grown up together in a small village and know each other like brothers and sisters. Like, it makes it a bit of a yawn." [17]

GArea smirks. "Those flowering bedrooms could be pretty quiet for a few years. At that age, some teens may just wanna sleep."

WSpace twists her torso to get a stretch in, reaching behind her on either side. "And there's no word about any natural birth control methods the Mosuo may have, any tips and techniques passed down by the elders. If they're into that sort of thing."

BSwan and GArea both nod, GArea adding, "an owner's manual to go along with the keys to the flowering bedroom."

"We haven't talked about the Mosuo economy either," WSpace continues. "A big part of what makes this culture work, is the family, the 'Firm.' Everyone has a role. Everybody works so they all have enough to eat. There's a real fine balance and they all know it.

"The absence of fathers and husbands isn't the same as in the West," she adds. "It's just comparing apples and oranges. In the West, when the male's missing it's a big gap.

"There isn't always an extended family to take over - even friends and neighbours. His absence affects the couple's economic situation. If the mother has to get extra employment (she may already be working), it affects care of children and the elderly."

"So, the more we think about the Mosuo way," GArea muses, "we shift our perspective. They do some positive things, pretty innovative, a few dozen centuries in the making."

BSwan leans over to pour more steaming tea. "I'm also thinking like they wouldn't have some of our you know challenging mental health issues: isolation, loneliness, right? And it could be pretty natural to be more considerate of the whole family."

WSpace nods, also reaching for a mug. "Naka's cousin Dawa talks about how being just a couple makes them a bit self-centred."

"The older Mosuo generation couldn't have seen the modern world coming," BSwan says sadly, taking a long sip. "They have every right to be sort of worried about what will happen to them. Who's to know? How do they prepare?"

The three fall quiet, contemplating a culture so different from their own. They add the role of life experience to their list of what's important to understand about other people to get along: values, expectations, and fears.

As they wrap up, BSwan reaches for headphones and leans back with eyes closed, listening to a catchy rhythm and guitar riff about walking in someone else's shoes.

* * *

REVIEW:

1. What do you think are the pros and cons of the Mosuo family culture when it comes to getting along with others? Explain.

2. The older Mosuo are concerned about how the old ways will be passed down to the next generation. What would you say to them?

3. How important is "making a name" for yourself in the Mosuo culture? Explain.

4. What are the Mosuo core values? Explain your choice.

THREE DESTINIES

PREVIEW:

1. To what extent are the opinions of young people and older people important? Explain.

* * *

SURVIVAL OF THE USEFUL: ICE AGE TIPS

The drone dips down through trees to a clearing and hovers over a group. A family in France is on an outing with lots of toys, play and drawing with ochre. Someone to one side is making a tool, then moves to another person maybe for advice before going back to their tool project.

It's the Ice Age. An estimated 40 to 60 per cent of its people were young and just learning community skills but still expected to help where needed. Modern-day archeologists suggest young people living in the Ice Age would engage most with elders whose teaching made the most sense.

If so, Ice Age young people might have had a big effect on the knowledge passed to the next generation, what was immediately useful, what continued to work and what didn't, in a survival or elimination of culture.[1]

* * *

REVIEW:

1. The Ice Age young people may have had what core value?
2. Give an example from your own life when you made a choice based on what you thought was useful and practical.

From Sichuan over the ancient city of Xi-an, Inner Mongolia, and Manchuria, the drone roars full throttle northeast over the Sea of Okhotsk and Bering Sea, the wind whistling. Through the windshield, the sun is blinding.

WSpace, GArea and BSwan keep GPS track of the route: over the Alaskan panhandle, down the West Coast of Turtle Island (British Columbia, Canada), gradually upward and inland, plateauing over the big lake, the melting of an ancient glacial icefield, the Okanagan Nation Syilx People's ancestral territory.

Here the drone drops in altitude over the surrounding dry hills and valley floor, hovering like a hummingbird. The click of seat belts fastened bounces off the walls. The drone sweeps to the left and right, gains altitude then takes a sudden dive for a closer look at the next set of perspectives.[2]

* * *

Her passion is her people, the Syilx of the Okanagan Nation,
uncovering the past to understand the present
and make a way forward.

ACADEMIC – ACTIVIST – ARTIST

PREVIEW:

1. What is art? What is activism? To what extent does art play a role in activism?

2. When two people of different cultures meet, how can they best get along?

3. Is there a "mystery gap" in knowledge of your culture? How might it be filled? Explain.

* * *

What motivates Jeannette Armstrong of the Okanagan Syilx Nation? What does her story have to say about getting along?

From a high school kid wanting to know more about her Okanagan language and heritage, to becoming the associate university professor she is today, Armstrong is all about digging deeper to find out more, then letting people know. Her passion is her people, the Syilx of the Okanagan Nation, uncovering the past to understand the present and make a way forward.

That high school kid started interpreting for elders, and was struck by how much they knew. On their part, the elders knew teaching young people was the future.

After her early studies at university, she got involved with school districts and wrote Indigenous curriculum, a time she recalled fondly. Armstrong zeroed in on her community's needs, how to strengthen traditional language in modern times, and the restorative role of Indigenous knowledge to heal damaged ecosystems. "We need to include as many pieces of knowledge from as many diverse corners of humanity," she said, "in order to solve this problem that seems not solvable." [1]

But Armstrong didn't just create classroom lessons. She wrote novels, poetry, and other works showing how an Indigenous person sees the world. Her first novel "Slash" (1985) sold more than 10,000 copies in Canada. It's the first-person account of a fictitious native man involved in the 1960s Red Power Movement, written for Grade 11 students, the first Canadian novel by an Indigenous woman.[2]

In her second novel "Whispering in Shadows" (2000), Penny the female activist character is weary. There is so much in society to correct.[3]

For Armstrong, art matters (and writing is art). Yes, it's inspiration tucked somewhere in consciousness, hovering, waiting to be given wings. It's also activism as expression, a life-line thrown to the next generation, giving voice and encouragement.

To that end, Armstrong has been heavily involved with the En'owkin Centre, which is operated by the six bands of the Okanagan Nation, and managed along with Okanagan College and the University of Victoria. It aims to give Indigenous students a strong cultural and academic foundation. Offshoots are Theytus Books Ltd (the first publishing house in Canada owned and operated by First Nations Peoples), and the En'owkin School of International Writing (the first creative writing school in Canada to award credit that is operated entirely for and by Aboriginal Peoples).[4]

Fast forward to recent years. The sun was shining. It was a UBC Okanagan convocation ceremony in Kelowna, British Columbia (University of British Columbia). Dr. Armstrong, wearing an Okanagan decorated cape and headpiece, carrying a large carved wooden paddle across her chest, led the faculty procession outdoors through the campus grounds. She stood tall, her eyes proud as she looked ahead in front of her. "To study in your language and your knowledge systems, which many English speakers take for granted, is not there for Indigenous Peoples," Dr. Armstrong said. "UBC Okanagan is at the cutting edge in making that breakthrough – it's a powerful statement of reconciliation." [5]

How did the first settlers get along with the Syilx? To find out, Armstrong and two UBCO colleagues dug deep into local records from the 1870's to 1960's. They were particularly interested in the relationship between women – settler and Syilx. What they found was striking. These early women did at times bond (many of whom were experienced horsewomen). Through

PART ONE - FAMOUS OR UNSUNG   49

their relationships (often due to inter-marriage, or a role as language interpreters) they gained insight into each other's culture. As a result of what they learned in general about each other, some tried to correct the public misconceptions.[6]

A daughter of Syilx parents wrote that a teepee is healthier than modern houses, providing fresh air. The Syilx suffered terribly, she said, by moving into houses. Indians also adopted poorer eating habits from settlers. More food doesn't necessarily mean more strength, she wrote, and overeating kills.[7]

From the perspective of another woman (daughter of a Syilx mother and settler father), settler and Syilx are intellectual equals. If anything, she stressed, the whites are hobbled by their writing and faith creeds. Indians have a more pared-down approach through their oral culture, she added, and it is more real.[8]

Dr. Jeannette Armstrong is an award-winning writer, activist, novelist and poet, recognized internationally. In 2016, Dr. Armstrong was named the first First Nations recipient of the George Woodcock Lifetime Achievement Award, British Columbia's most prestigious literary honour recognizing local authors.[9]

As a knowledge keeper of plant medicines, Syilx traditions and ways, Dr. Armstrong speaks the Syilx language fluently ("Nsyilxcn"). Armstrong is Associate Professor (Indigenous Studies) at the Irving K. Barber School of Arts and Sciences at UBC Okanagan. She holds a Canada Research Chair in Okanagan Indigenous Philosophy and, in 2021, was elected a Fellow in the Royal Society of Canada. She holds a PhD in Indigenous Environmental Ethics and Syilx Indigenous Oral Literature. Dr Armstrong was inducted into the Order of Canada as an officer in June 2023.[10]

* * *

"This is fascinating," GArea murmurs. "Jeannette Armstrong – I'll call her 'Dr. J' – is straddling two worlds: Western academia, and Indigenous knowledge keeper who is fluent in the Syilx language. We heard from the Himalayan grandfather that education disrupts village life, and from older Mosuo villagers that the modern world threatens their traditional culture.

"But here's Dr. J basically taking the attitude that she'll learn from both for the benefit of her community. Basically, she's setting the example of how it can work."

"Ya, she's kind of devoting her life to carrying her culture forward, picking it up and carrying it," BSwan says in wonder, leaning on elbows. "Like sort of caring for an injured animal on the roadway."

WSpace points out that Indigenous women have traditionally played key roles in community government and spiritual ceremony. In eastern Turtle Island (Canada), one 1742 French Jesuit missionary and ethnologist noted that Iroquois or "Haudenosaunee" women, similar to Genghis Khan's daughters, had the authority and maintained the tribe.[11]

"As for straddling academia and traditional knowledge," WSpace adds, filling a glass with water, "we also have that comment from an 1800's woman making a judgment: the whites are 'bound and limited' by their written culture. Indigenous people are 'closer to nature and reality.' So it really depends on what your attitude will be. Are you going to work with the differences, or not?" GArea and BSwan nod.

"In today's world," WSpace continues, "it seems pretty ironic that the culture of writing things down is playing a big role in keeping the oral Syilx culture alive, say at the En'owkin Centre. It's making it more accessible to more people."

"Ya, talk about that Ice Age idea of sort of survival of the most immediately useful," BSwan adds. "It's awesome how in today's world writing down an ancient culture is practical, useful right now."

"Getting along" for Dr. J appears to mean creating balance by showing the power of being an Indigenous person, the three decide, and supporting her Indigenous heritage in order for it to thrive going forward. Her first step was that she herself – and her Syilx community – had to know that heritage.

"I never realized how much that settlers and Syilx back in the 1800's were learning the other's language." GArea is impressed. "They really had to, to get things done. Back then, it seems there was more direct interaction. There was no highway or airport. Pack horse was the way in and out of the region."

"Once a settler woman got beyond thinking Syilx stories were just legend and folktale," WSpace was now leaning forward with quiet emphasis, "she began to see it was their way to tell important and wise lessons."

"A great way to keep the little kids interested," GArea laughs softly.

"...and the rest of us," WSpace adds pointedly with a smile.

PART ONE - FAMOUS OR UNSUNG

* * *

REVIEW:

1. What are Dr. Jeannette Armstrong's core values?

2. What aspect of Dr. Armstrong's work do you think is most important for Indigenous Peoples: academic? community activist? award-winning artist (writer)? Explain.

3. To what extent is the Okanagan Nation's En'owkin Centre bridging the gap between oral Indigenous culture and written settler culture? Explain.

What he learned about being self-sufficient by earning a paycheque has stayed useful his whole life, and is the theme of his leadership.

MARKETPLACE MOJO:TALL AGAIN IN THE SADDLE

PREVIEW:

1. How did you earn your first money? What did you do with it? How did you feel?
2. What does it mean to have a "thick skin"? a "thin skin"? Explain.

* * *

The small room was filling with people finding empty seats among the rows of chairs. I'm in my mid-30s in my first few years as a full-time daily newspaper reporter in the South Okanagan. The session was ready to begin. The organizer acknowledged a slight-built young man in the back obscured from my view, with a fine-featured poker face that revealed nothing. It's Chief Clarence Louie of the Osoyoos Indian Band (OIB). To this day, I recall my surprise. This "K'il law na" grizzly bear (Louie's ancestral name means strength and determination)[1] was unobtrusive, unassuming, silently taking everything in.

In 1905, a Norwegian teenager dreamed of a bicycle. In the 1970s, 16-year-old Clarence Louie dreamed of a fast car and what it represented: independence and having something of his own, making a name for himself among the kids at the local largely white high school, building a reputation, respect, and fitting in. While the Norwegian left his country in pursuit of the bicycle, Louie, over the years since the 70's, made his name by focusing on his Okanagan Syilx community at the northern tip of the Sonoma Desert (just south of Jeannette Armstrong's home reserve). By doing so, it's the outside world that has come to Louie and the OIB. He's been Chief since 1984 when he was first elected at 24 years old.[2]

As a young teenager, what impressed Louie as most immediately useful was the power of making his own money (marketplace currency), beginning as a pre-teen in the OIB's vineyard, then through a summer job at Kootenay National Park. What he learned about being self-sufficient by earning a paycheque has stayed useful his whole life, the theme of his leadership. According to Louie, Indigenous people are no strangers to hard work and the marketplace. They've been entrepreneurs for thousands of years, and need to again take control of their economic life to regain self-pride and self-respect. First Nations succeed in the modern world by taking personal responsibility.[3]

Leadership is crucial. Being the elected chief and council on a First Nations "Rez" isn't easy, Louie said, because rez politics tends to be tense with greed and internal squabbles common ("reserve" in Canada, and "reservation" in the U.S.). Think more sour than sweet, tough than tender. As Louie said in his book "Rez Rules: My Indictment of Canada's and America's Systemic Racism Against Indigenous Peoples", it's more like a TV family that's rough around the edges.[4]

Over the years, Louie and council members - past and present - have created a prosperous community where there's two job opportunities for every band member. The best model for kids, Louie said, is parents who have a job. Based on its population (per capita basis), the OIB has more businesses and joint ventures than any other First Nation in Canada.[5]

As with each of his council colleagues, Louie has only one vote on band council so he presents his thoughts on particular issues then lets councillors make their own decisions.

He has built a reputation for speaking his mind and seeking solutions in the wider community for the good of his Indigenous home reserve. Louie makes it work. How did other "whistle blowers" fare in the past - both Indigenous and settler - when they spoke their mind? Not well, according to Bob Joseph, author of "21 Things You May Not Know About the Indian Act: Helping Canadians Make Reconciliation with Indigenous Peoples a Reality." Here's two examples:

Dr. Peter Bryce, Chief Medical Officer "Medical Inspector" (Canadian departments of the Interior and Indian Affairs) – In 1907, after visiting 35 residential schools, Bryce reported unsanitary conditions, lack of ventilation, and high death rates most likely due to tuberculosis. His recommendations for improvement were ignored by the federal government.[6]

Lieutenant Frederick Loft (Mohawk, Six Nations Band) – Four thousand Indigenous people fought overseas on behalf of Canada during World War I (1914-1918), despite not being considered "people" under the law. The reason they went to war may have been because they were concerned about war affecting their treaty rights, or they thought there would be better conditions as a soldier than back home on their reserve. In any case, they decided they all had poor conditions back home. Loft took the problem to the Privy Council and the King of England. Nothing much happened. Loft also liked the idea of a League of Indians in Canada. After the war, he brought Chiefs together for annual meetings. Loft asked the Chiefs for a fee to send native young people to high school. The federal government apparently didn't think it was a good idea. The 1927 Indian Act made it illegal for Indigenous Peoples to form a political organization. Loft and the Chiefs didn't try to formally organize again until World War II.[7]

Times have changed. How to get along together in today's world, and lessen conflicts? Louie has learned from many people. Among other points, strong leadership the Chief Louie way means:

1.***Develop a thick skin.*** Don't take criticism personally, and don't be afraid to stand alone if you believe something strongly. As a 17-year-old high school student, Louie organized everything on a sports team from player scheduling to tournaments. He learned how to get along with a wide variety of people to meet a goal (Ask yourself: What's going on here? What's the group dynamic?). Louie learned to recognize the politics of criticism, and how to handle it. Criticism is cheap and easy, and an organizer will often be the target. Others may complain but few will step up to help out. Watch out for the people who never appear to be satisfied. They will drain you.[8]

2.***Don't be shy. Connect with people.*** Go to the people in the know, and learn from them. When Louie was still in his 30's, he brought to a Chiefs' Business Summit one of the province's most well-known business figures: Jimmy Pattison. At another time, he invited to the OIB the Harvard Project on American Indian Economic Development. Harvard University professor

Steve Cornell explained to the OIB the Harvard findings over 30 years that showed how some First Nations succeed and others don't. Later, the OIB held visioning workshops to set future goals. Work together. Build relationships, partnerships, alliances. Help each other. (Remember how Genghis Khan depended on his Mongol queens.) Pick up the phone and call, text or email; it may only take a few minutes. Be open to new information, and be willing to change your mind. Keep learning. Leaders are readers (including audiobooks, e-books, podcasts and videos).[9]

3.**Set up a system that supports your group.** Be professional. Do it right. Pin down group rules. Organize so everyone can see what's happening, with help to be responsible, accountable, and transparent. Delegate and let others do their job. Encourage group members to bring up any concerns, with evidence. When the voting is for a controversial issue, set up a secret ballot.[10]

4.**Take responsibility for yourself.** Be dependable. Be on time (prompt, punctual). Work hard (with measurable results). Be low-maintenance (and work with what you have). Don't demand special treatment.

5.**Be respectful and build trust.** It doesn't take much to ruin a relationship. Scold with humility. It's never okay to call someone bad names. Set feelings aside for the good of all.[11]

Chief Clarence Louie holds two honorary doctorates (from the University of British Columbia, and Queen's University, both 2021), as well as an Order of British Columbia, and Order of Canada (2016), the country's highest civilian honour. In 2013, MacLean's magazine named him one of the "top 50 Canadians to watch." He's the first Indigenous person to be inducted into the Canadian Business Hall of Fame (2019), and was also named the Ernst and Young Entrepreneur of the Year (2008). Previously, in 2003 Louie was one of six First Nations leaders the U.S. Department of State asked to review economic development in American Indian communities.[12]

* * *

"You're late!" GArea's voice reverberates around the drone's central work area. "I was researching, and my daughter called me," WSpace sputters as she pops out of her pod, pulls the screen down behind her, and heads to the kitchen for ginger tea and an oatmeal raisin cookie from a bin.

GArea gives an exasperated deep exhale. "I hate it when people are late."

"Hilarious! You sound like Chief Clarence Louie, ya?" BSwan laughs, looking up from a brightly lit phone, headphones over ears. Apparently GArea is loud enough to be heard.

"Well, Louie has a good point," GArea turns his head sharply. "People in general, not just some First Nations people, don't respect other people's time."

WSpace takes a seat and opens her laptop. "That whole 'making a name for yourself' idea again, and focusing on what's most useful. It's so human. Especially for young people just starting their lives. For Louie, it's all tied in with earning cash. How powerful must it have been to buy a cool car?"

"The Indigenous in Canada before residential schools went sour, and the Maragoli in Kenya both had the same idea after World War I," GArea muses. "Both figured their kids needed educating in white settler ways to be ready for the new wage economy." [13] He heads for a mug of coffee, takes a cookie and drops back into his seat. "A kid learns that some sweat equity on his part gets him what he wants in life. Combine that with meeting people and building connections, and Louie was on his way."

"Seriously!" BSwan is eyeing GArea's cookie. "He's a hard worker, right? He knows how to sort of organize things and people to get things done. And he's learned how to read people, to figure them out."

"Not just to read *people* but to read, *period*." GArea moves his cookie closer to himself. "He's able to reach a lot of his goals by researching and finding things out."

"And imagine having a birth name that means 'grizzly'? "WSpace chuckles. "What would that do to your sense of being tenacious, thick-skinned, tough? Something to live up to.

"Being a whistle blower, and speaking your mind," she adds. "The times have really changed. Bryce and Loft could have done some real good, too, could have changed history, if they'd been given a chance. But it wasn't meant to be."

PART ONE - FAMOUS OR UNSUNG

"No, the time wasn't quite right, sadly," GArea agrees. "Even in today's world, Louie stresses how important it is to have a really thick skin. You have to not let criticism and setbacks bring you down, but stay focused."

GArea hoists himself up, shuffles to the kitchen, takes another cookie from the bin and plunks it down in front of BSwan.

* * *

REVIEW:

1. What are Chief Clarence Louie's core values? Explain your choices.

2. To what extent do you agree with Louie that the best model for kids is to see their parents with a job?

3. Three people here "speak their mind." Who are they, what did they say, and what happened as a result?

4. What five points does Louie make about strong leadership?

The fact remains, she said, that long-lasting cooperation is more difficult than conflict.

MOJAG HIJINKS WITH JUSTIN AND JODY

PREVIEW:

1. What does it mean to be "pushed into a corner"? Have you ever been there? Explain.

2. Have you ever felt alone in sticking up for what you thought was right? How did it feel?

* * *

The drone leaves the inland lakes and the dry valley bottom behind, rising high above coastal mountains before diving down to the sea, heading north up the inland strait then across to the big island.

Gentle water laps against the shoreline, a seagull picking through debris. Another calls overhead, wheeling back and forth through the mist, diving then soaring higher.

It's the West Coast, land of salmon and cedar, totem poles and potlatch celebration. This is Jody Wilson-Raybould's home, village life couched in rainforest silence.

A voice echoes down through the years. B.C. First Nations Hereditary Chief and Aboriginal spokesperson Bill Wilson sits across from then Prime Minister Pierre Elliott Trudeau during the 1983 constitutional talks surrounded by men, steady gaze meeting steady gaze. Wilson tells Trudeau his two young daughters dream of being lawyers and Prime Minister one day. The men around them guffaw. Trudeau says he'll wait. Wilson has the final punch line, saying the B.C. government could fly them to Ottawa that evening. The crowd erupts in laughter.[1]

Family legacy. Reputation. Expectations.

At the time, Jody was a Grade 6 student at Comox Elementary School on Vancouver Island. Fast forward 32 years to 2015. Trudeau's oldest son Justin was Prime Minister. He appointed Wilson-Raybould the first

Aboriginal Minister of Justice and Attorney General (MOJAG), the Crown's chief law officer. She had been Regional Chief of the B.C. Assembly of First Nations for two terms, a Councillor for the We Wai Kai Nation, a chair of the First Nations Finance Authority, an aboriginal advocate, lawyer and British Columbia Crown prosecutor.[2]

As she relayed in her 2021 memoir "'Indian' in the Cabinet: Speaking Truth to Power," Wilson-Raybould was born and bred to take on a key leadership role among Canadian Indigenous Peoples. The time appeared right to take her extensive training and experience to another level to Canadian federal politics, and a culture new to her.

By the time she left national politics six years later, she was deeply disillusioned. She'd hoped for more action, greater change. Her father had worked hard to clarify protections for the rights of Indigenous Peoples, and the inherent right of self-government. Protection of Indigenous rights in the Constitution has made a difference, she agreed. However, what now needs to happen, she said, is for the federal government to build in the space and support to allow Indigenous Peoples - at various stages of preparedness across the country - to rebuild their own communities to meet their own needs their way in their own time. For that to happen, she said, the existing Indian Act must go.[3]

Traditional Indigenous worldviews and customs, she said, must be present in all aspects of Indigenous community life: education, healthcare, family protection services, economy, environment, culture, language. The United Nations Declaration on the Rights of Indigenous Peoples (UNDRIP) shows the way. Canada needs to follow it, create national policy, and take strong action. At the same time, she said, some Indigenous Peoples still prefer on-going negotiation, and struggle with the right way forward for themselves.[4]

Interpersonal communication can be complex and challenging, Wilson-Raybould agreed, and each person plays a role in the outcome. She recognized that being single-minded, with an agenda and time-frame can create tension with others. Wilson-Raybould said she sees herself as a proud Canadian intent on balance in her work in government and also with Indigenous Peoples across Canada, helping people come together to shift perspective. Sometimes it means pushing hard. Balance is key in her Indigenous heritage, and women play a crucial role.[5]

It was the SNC-Lavalin firestorm, not Indigenous issues as such, that lead to Wilson-Raybould leaving the Trudeau Liberal government. SNC-Lavalin is a global engineering and construction firm based in Montreal (with a workforce of approximately 9,000 across Canada, and 50,000 worldwide).[6] It faced fraud and bribery charges regarding a contract in Libya.

Was the director of public prosecution correct to begin legal proceedings against SNC-Lavalin? Or should SNC-Lavalin have been given some time to make things right? It was Wilson-Raybould's job to decide, as Attorney-General (the Crown's independent top law officer). Wilson-Raybould investigated and decided the director had made an appropriate decision. The criminal case against SNC-Lavalin would go ahead without delay. Wilson-Raybould claimed she was pressured by the Liberal government to go easy on SNC-Lavalin and give a cooling-off period. At one point, Wilson-Raybould taped a phone conversation with a high government official for evidence.[7]

Later, In December 2018, SNC-Lavalin pled guilty to a single count of fraud, and was fined $280 million. The company did not move from Canada, and did not lay-off a substantial number of workers. Wilson-Raybould claimed the government did no analysis regarding the potential for job loss. At the time, CBC News senior investigative correspondent Diana Swain also found no evidence that SNC-Lavalin's ongoing Canadian project commitments were in danger, or that SNC would move its head office from Montreal.[8]

Looking back at her time in office, Wilson-Raybould said she's proud of her efforts to improve the Canadian legal system's treatment of Indigenous Peoples. She's proud of her 250 appointments of new judges to fill vacancies, appointments that reflect multicultural diversity.[9]

Yes, she could have been more strategic, cooperative, flexible, she said. However, she feels it wouldn't have made much of a difference - other than turning down the heat a bit on Indigenous and justice issues for all involved. The fact remains, she said, that long-lasting cooperation is more difficult than conflict.[10]

After serving as the minister of justice and attorney general of Canada, the minister of veterans affairs, and the associate minister of national defence, Jody Wilson-Raybould resigned from Cabinet in 2019. Wilson-Raybould continued as an Independent member of Parliament and was re-elected in 2019 as the Independent MP for Vancouver Granville. She chose not to run for office in 2021.[11]

* * *

Thud, Thud, Thud, Thud. Limp hair is plastered to GArea's forehead, sweat trickling down his cheeks, his face ruddy with exertion.

For the past hour, GArea has been plodding along heavily on the treadmill in the far corner going nowhere, mopping his forehead with the white towel draped around his neck, his eyes glued to the scene unfolding out the drone window. Next to him, BSwan is hunkered over the stationary bike, leaning on elbows, legs spinning furiously.

WSpace is sprawled on a blue mat in the middle of the floor, stretching one leg over another, craning the other arm, her head, shoulders and back in the opposite direction. Holding. Breathing slowly and quietly. "Okay, let's go," she says.

The three move to the table, rub sore muscles, fill glasses with water, and stare at the huge mound of salad greens and vegetables in a large bowl, dried cranberries, and char-grilled salmon fillets. "Hmmm..." They fill plates, and get to work.

"I think she shouldn't have taped that conversation, without letting the other guy know she was doing it." GArea starts. His fork stabs into the salad. WSpace is savoring a bite of salmon. "That's your opinion. Go on."

"You're always talking about the need to give the other person space," he looks up. "She may have felt pushed into a corner, but it's important to separate the two." BSwan nods, fork in mouth.

"So what's at stake here?" WSpace digs deeper, reaching for her laptop, pen and paper. "First of all, we have the technology to record anyone and anything most anytime. I'm thinking that, even during a business call, a company will often say if the call is being recorded 'for training purposes'."

"Exactly!" GArea nods emphatically. "Otherwise, it feels like surveillance, spying. Not the base for any kind of transparency and trust."

BSwan looks thoughtful, and leans on one hand. "Ya, I think that the thing, too, is that it becomes a sort of lopsided conversation, right? She knows it's being recorded. He doesn't. I'm thinking that it's bound to affect what she says, even if she thinks she's speaking naturally."

"Your opinion. Okay." WSpace shifts in her chair. "That idea of feeling pushed into a corner. It seems she was really feeling pressured, frustrated, and having a hard time getting in to the Prime Minister to talk about it. Sounds like she was very upset at what she felt was interference in her independence as the Attorney General."

BSwan leans forward. "Right, and sounds like she was also feeling sort of labeled as an Indigenous person: second class, an outsider on Parliament Hill."

GArea cuts in, "And maybe feeling that decisions were being made around her without her input. Really feeling the effects of a lack of transparency, lack of trust. Aha!" He leans back, "We're back to where we started. It seems she apparently felt a lack of transparency and trust in her dealings with the PMO (Prime Minister's office). So it seems she retaliated with a move that unfortunately might breed more lack of transparency and trust."

"Hmm," WSpace leans over to pull out her knitting. "I'm thinking that a knee-jerk reaction when we feel under attack can be really damaging. It can add to the problem. Wilson-Raybould says herself that cooperation is not easy."

The three agree that Wilson-Raybould's frustrations were understandable. On a larger scale, in thinking of the other issue of reconciliation with Indigenous Peoples in general, the drone team also agreed that reconciliation is uncharted territory full of thorns. There's no clear way forward.

"We have done hard things before," BSwan smiles ruefully, meaningfully.

"Obama at 2021? COP Glasgow?" WSpace pauses. BSwan nods.[12]

Talk turns to what Dr. Jeannette Armstrong, Chief Clarence Louie, and Jody Wilson-Raybould contribute in their own ways to getting along. While Dr. J appears most comfortable sharing what she's unearthed from the past and supports a future Indigenous voice, Louie is making economic connections, and ensures his one council vote makes a difference.

Wilson-Raybould, on the other hand, took that networking to parliament, on an even more public stage.

Whether it be academia, activism, art. Entrepreneurial economic development. Or the political arena, the legal system. All play a part to further Indigenous rights. Being Indigenous is not "one size fits all."

"You know." WSpace lays down her knitting, and contemplates the work, the goals of Armstong, Louie and Wilson-Raybould. "I'm thinking how important it is for anyone with a mission to go slow to go fast, to get things done in the long run.

"It seems that with the whole sense of a destiny with Justin and Jody expectations were really over the top. I'm thinking that expectations can really get in the way of seeing the other person as they are," WSpace looks GArea and BSwan in the eye. They nod. "So many of these stories are about people making their way, making a name, building a reputation. 'Who am I, and who do I want to be?'" GArea is gazing out the window and adds, "'Who are my people, and who do we want to be? What do we do here, and what do we want to do?'"

"Absolutely." BSwan looks longingly at the last piece of salmon in the bowl. "And it seems I guess the lesson is also to sort of be careful of expectations. You know, Seneca the Roman Stoic philosopher had a great quote about that. 'Expecting is the greatest impediment to living. In anticipation of tomorrow, it loses today.'" [13]

* * *

REVIEW:

1. What do you think about Jody Wilson-Raybould's reasons for audiotaping a conversation without telling the other person? Explain.

2. Regarding her time as MOJAG, what is Wilson-Raybould most proud of?

3. According to Wilson-Raybould, what is more important than fighting for a cause?

4. What are Wilson-Raybould's core values? Explain.

CHAPTER THREE -
Everyday Aggravation

"I'm not going to stand back and watch that happen. Not me."

THE BIG "TRY" - WALKING THEM IN

PREVIEW:

1. Think of a time when you gave extra support to someone. How did it feel?
2. Think of a time when you got extra support from someone. How did it feel?

* * *

The drone retraced its flight inland in time for the big event. Hovering particularly high over the dry South Okanagan hills, all that WSpace, GArea and BSwan saw out the front windshield were what looked like very busy ants spread out over the valley floor: the runners and cyclists, bystanders and aid station volunteers.

It's an amazing test of physical stamina in the same 17-hour day - a 3.8-kilometer swim (2.4 miles), 180-kilometer bike race (112 miles), and 42-kilometer marathon run (26 miles). (The clock starts first thing in the morning when the athlete enters the water.)[1]

Over the years, triathlon events around the world have attracted top-flight athletes as well as novices just learning to swim. Thousands start the day with the hope of a run to the finish line before the cut-off time, cheers from onlookers, and the announcer shouting their names as successful finishers.

Many spectators volunteered at aid stations along the route, then headed to the finish line in time to welcome the first finishers, top athletes in their age categories. Others like Mark (not his real name) volunteered for six hours, then made sure they were at the finish line the last hour before cut-off. Mark joined the raucous family and friends lining the route clanking cow bells. The last of the athletes struggled to finish.

"I find it very fun to encourage the people to finish and even do a run in on the final straightaway," Mark said.[2] At times, there were tears in his solemn eyes. He's a heavyset guy. Over the years he himself had physical challenges yet made impressive comebacks. He's pushed his body to accomplish long-distance goals.

Mark knew when it was time to get off the bleachers and briskly walk the few meters to the corner where he stood among onlookers. The last 30 minutes, Mark was on the lookout for the last runner of the day, taking a personal interest. "I don't think she's going to make it," or "He's not looking too good."

He peered into the dark down the road, waiting, gritting his teeth. "I just like to see everyone come in."

"Runner!" he barked to the dwindling crowd, as the last runner came into view. The runner took the corner so close to the nearby finish line, then headed away down along the lake boardwalk to begin the last stretch out and back. Very few bystanders had Mark's commitment. In the dark, he headed down the course after the runner, to meet this last one's return. There was only a handful of onlookers out here, mostly a couple of the runner's immediate circle, witnesses of support. And Mark. It's quiet. Most of the cowbells are gone.

He walked alongside the struggling athlete who was still jogging, or at a steady painful walk. Mark quietly offered encouragement, even when it was clear the runner wouldn't make the cut-off time. For Mark, it was deeply satisfying.

The next day, he drove the five hours back down to the Coast. Then it was another three-hour trip by ferry back home to the Island. The last triathletes had hoped to meet the 17-hour cutoff. Mark knew he made a difference to the ones who needed it most.

* * *

Tissues fly from the box in the center of the table, a soft exhale as one-by-one WSpace, GArea, and BSwan reach across and yank out one or two. WSpace dabs sheepishly at her eyes, and casts a sideways glance at the others. BSwan does the same.

But GArea is openly weeping, leaning on the table, and supporting his forehead in one hand. He mops his sopping eyes, blows his nose with a honk, pulls another tissue. He honks again forcefully then absently wipes his eyes as WSpace stares. "I don't know why this one's got to me."

Gradually the sobs subside. BSwan gets up, walks to the kitchenette, and brings back three steaming cups of tea. "Thank you, Swan," GArea sighs, breathing deeply. WSpace leans over and squeezes GArea's arm.

"We've been under a lot of strain, working really hard, trying to understand why people do what they do," she murmurs looking into his eyes. "There's a lot at stake. You're allowed to vent, GArea."

"I feel like an idiot," he sniffs.

"No, no." WSpace shakes her head emphatically. "Don't talk like that."

For a few minutes, the three sit in silence, taking long gulps of tea. BSwan sits hunched over a cup. "Should we break 'er down?" BSwan says finally, lifting eyes. WSpace glances at GArea who nods. "Ya."

She reaches for a pen and paper. "Let's do it."

"What makes us so emotional about this one?" WSpace muses. "It's a short little story, but so powerful." The three of them mull it over. What they come up with is empathy. "For this guy, the whole triathlon thing represents something more." GArea has regained his composure, and pushes up his sleeves before leaning forward, hand gesticulating in the air.

"He's looking beyond the competitive race aspect. What really gets him is the struggle from the unlikely participants." WSpace nods. "They don't know the outcome, but they're striving anyway to do something really difficult."

"Ya, exactly," BSwan is nodding excitedly. "It's that relating deep in your gut to that kind of 'oh my god, I don't know if I can do this!' you know and wanting to help." It's when a person opens up and is vulnerable that magic happens. Others either turn away in embarrassment because the spectacle is too scary or like Mark they step up, link arms, and get involved.

"The tears come," GArea pauses as if he's just had an insight. "Seeing someone else be really vulnerable just grabs your own emotions."

"Alright, then." WSpace is writing furiously. "So what does this tell us about getting along?"

"If we can tap into how others are trying, and support it somehow, we're doing all we can to work together," GArea muses.

"It helps us in our own hurt, to help others in theirs. We try to fill the gap in support, ya that's it!" BSwan leans back in triumph.

"Who knows what Mark's motivation is," GArea muses. "Some past experience when he felt helpless to help. Not wanting that to happen again. A need to be different than everybody else. To be significant. To have a role to play. Saying to himself 'I'm not going to stand back and watch that happen, not me.'"

WSpace's pen bobs up and down as her list grows: "Open yourself to do something you're not sure of, something hard. Take a risk. Share your vulnerability. See your own vulnerable self in others. Acknowledge their efforts. Be supportive. Even if it means going out of your way to travel cross-province to be the only one left to walk in with the last struggling triathlon runner."

* * *

REVIEW:

1. What was Mark's goal at the triathlon event? To what extent do you think his goal is important? Explain.

2. What is Mark's core value? Explain your choice. a) winning b) being fit c) support d) looking good e) being fast f) technique g) getting along, or?

3. GArea was embarrassed about crying. However, using the word "idiot" was somewhat insensitive. How?

*WSpace was wildly shaking her hands in front of her
as if wringing the two men's necks.*

TEACHER RUMBLE

PREVIEW:

1. Why is it better to use "I" instead of "you" when you're having a difficult conversation with someone?
2. Why is it often better to include a third party to help you work through your difficult conversation?

* * *

"I'm out a year's salary because of you." "Is that so? You have no idea what it's like to be the person in charge. You're naïve." The two educators up on the drone screen were both in attack mode.

As mediator, WSpace had begun this session calm, composed and confident with a plan in mind. But after hearing their opening comments, her cheeks were flushed, her breathing shallow. She could feel her stomach, throat and jaw tighten. Sitting at the drone table, White Space's hair in front of her forehead was messed from her leaning forward on one hand, as she looked down at the papers scattered around her. This was the story.

At the end of the school year, teacher Kye had been deeply offended by the actions of principal Gillies, and decided to not return. Kye couldn't see himself staying for another year. It was a tough decision. Both Kye and Gillies had sent a written statement to WSpace. Now it was time to talk together. Kye was first.

"You didn't seem to know how to work with us for the good of everybody. You made decisions at a moment's notice, then you wondered why we were upset. No explanation except to blame everyone else. Definitely not a diplomat.

"You took offense if we questioned you. Anyone else doing a good job? That was a big threat to you. And you got way too strict with the kids. If they had some ideas to make things better? No pat on the back from you.

"I want you to take some responsibility for what happened. I want us to sit down and hash this over. I'm up for it. Are you?"

On the principal's part, Gillies was equally blunt. "The kids will run wild unless you rein them in. They've gotta follow the rules. Administration wanted a tight ship, and they finance the school. There was no time to consult with everyone and get everyone's opinion. I've gotta respond quickly and change things. That's just the way it is in a school. I'm the one meeting with students, staff, support staff, admin, parents. I'm the one everyone comes to with their complaints.

"I needed you as a teacher to do what I say. You criticized me in front of the whole school. That wasn't right. I couldn't trust you; maybe you were after my job. You made me look bad. Literally! All that physical exercise you did. Really? I had to cut you down.

"You brought it all on yourself. You didn't know how to play the game and make the principal look good. That's what you're supposed to do if you wanna get ahead."

"Cut!" WSpace roared, startling the two men into silence. "Alright, you two, take a break. Who are you talking about?" Kye and Gillies looked at her blankly. "What do you mean 'who'?" [1]

"You heard me," WSpace's shoulders were pulled back, her chest high. "Are you talking about yourself or the other person? Who's the focus?" They still looked blank. Impatiently, WSpace sighed. "The pronoun! Are you talking about 'I' or 'you'?"

"You," Kye murmured quickly.

"Exactly! You this, you that. Big mistake. Right away you're putting the other person on the defensive. You're even telling the other person what they were thinking, feeling! Why they did what they did! As if you knew." WSpace guffawed loudly in disgust.

From their individual screens, the two men looked uncomfortable, fidgeted awkwardly in their chairs, and avoided WSpace's eyes.

"What I want you to do," she leaned forward, and spoke slowly, deliberately, "is focus on 'I' when you're making your points. Talk about what you know for sure: your own feelings, and thoughts. Start again."[2] The two looked at the statements in front of them. "Wait! Five steps. I want you to talk in five steps. Get out a pen and paper."

Kye and Gillies halted – their eyes frozen on WSpace – then slowly blinked, breathed, and leaned to either side of the screen for a pen and notepad.

"Before you speak, make a plan. It doesn't have to be a big deal. But focus first. Number one: think before you speak. Number two: what's the other person's viewpoint? Find out! Once you have that, is there anything at all you can apologize for?"[3]

Gillies' eyes went hard. He leaned forward to speak, but WSpace interrupted.

"Yes, I mean an honest apology. Find something you can honestly apologize for, even if it's something small. Number three: what's the real problem between you that's led to this conflict? Figure it out together."

WSpace was wildly shaking her hands in front of her as if wringing the two men's necks. "Now, where's the compromise? How can you meet the other person in the middle, to meet each of your needs?"

Gillies went back to his scribbling. Kye's head was bent low over his own notepad.

"What we're working towards here is some sort of resolution. That's number four: stay calm. Together, can you find a potential solution that both of you can at least live with? Once you're there, it's time for number five: end on a positive note. Basically, say how you value the other person, your relationship."

Kye looked ill. WSpace marched on, "Say how glad you are that together you figured out a solution, if you ARE glad of course. Be honest."

The look Kye and Gillies gave each other was deeply restrained, like two reptiles ready to strike. They weren't ready yet to play nice. They had work to do to get there, but they were thinking about WSpace's words. WSpace herself had perked up. As she gathered and sorted her papers, she looked energized and resolute, sitting taller, her head held high, ready to resume the process.

"Look guys," she added. "You also know, don't you, that your words are only a small part of the story?" Gillies and Kye again looked blank.

Body language doesn't lie. It reveals all, WSpace stressed. True feelings show in the body, face, voice tone, and how assertive a person appears. Try to be calm and look ready to talk. "Look the other person in the eye.

Acknowledge their points with a nod or two. Keep your physical distance – give them space, don't fidget. Be interested and concerned about the other person's point of view, their mood." [4]

WSpace glanced at a list of common co-worker behaviors, from back-stabber to criticizer, ethics violator to mistake-maker, or Negative Ned. She wondered which ones fit Kye and Gillies. Then there were the 10 boss types: from abusive to incompetent, inconsistent to reactive. [5] Time would tell. She was thinking ahead – with not a little apprehension - to the next session with Gillies and Kye.

The next morning, the sun was just showing its face in a clear blue sky, over the far mountains. The three gathered again for what promised to be a long day of talking and listening. Gillies, Kye and WSpace were each in their places, showered, hair neatly combed and brushed.

The first to speak could be the one who would take the lead in the discussion, and admit that something needed to change. Kye began, looking Gillies straight in the camera.

"Gillies, thanks for doing this. You're busy." Gillies' shoulders softened slightly. He was listening, also looking directly at Kye. The corners of WSpace's mouth lifted a little.

"I didn't want to leave the school." Kye paused and exhaled deeply. Something within him loosened. "I'm sorry it came to that.

"I could have been more tactful. I needed to switch how I talked with you. You were my boss, and I needed to talk to you that way. I should have brought things up in private.

"I was frustrated when I saw more strictness. I didn't see collaboration. I thought we all could have worked together better for the good of everybody. It didn't have to take a lot of time. This is what I was seeing: secretive behavior, unilateral decisions behind people's backs, disrespect. If you want, we can talk about specific incidents."

"I can't comment on anyone else but me, because I'm not them. I only know what my own reactions were." Kye glanced at WSpace with a childlike glint in his eye. The corners of her eyes and mouth lifted even more.

"I want to understand how this happened," Kye continued. "I thought that by being honest I was supporting you. I thought I was helping you to see gaps, to build a better school environment. I wasn't questioning your ability as principal. We both know you're a very capable, hard-working educator." Kye finished simply. "What do you think?"

WSpace called for a break, and the screens went black. She walked to the drone kitchen for hot water and a tea bag, impressed with how Kye had switched from the accusations of his earlier written statement. She saw how he was now focusing on "I" talk.

When the session resumed, Gillies sat silent for several moments looking off to one side, before he began.

"Kye, you've been a good friend, and I'd like to say I was glad to meet with you to talk about this. But if we're being honest here, the truth is I find it hard to do, the 'talking-it-over' bit."

Gillies was still leaning to one side, looking off in the distance to one corner of his laptop screen, his face impassive. Kye glanced up, his mouth slightly open. WSpace paused in her note-taking.

"If this all didn't happen, it would have meant less work for me, that's for sure." Gillies gave the slightest of a wry laugh, took a breath, and sat up straighter in his chair. "Thank you, WSpace, for your help. I had a lot on my plate. I wanted to do a good job." Gillies began to look uncomfortable and to fidget.

"This is gonna sound like making excuses, but nothing's come easy for me. It's been a battle." Gillies was scratching at a mark on the table. A sun-lit window to one side of him left his face in partial shadow.

"So looking back that year, being principal could be snatched away at any moment and I couldn't let that happen." Gillies stopped, looking down. Then he straightened. "You're a very capable teacher, very confident speaking in a group. When you criticized me, especially in front of others, I took it very personally." There was no sound, no movement. "I felt I couldn't trust you. We were friends, but I thought you weren't on my side anymore."

WSpace let the silence sit in the air then spoke softly. "Thank you, Gillies." Kye was looking down at his own feet, his shoulders slumped.

"Gentlemen, we've addressed steps one and two. Now we need to pin down the core issue. What exactly went wrong?" After talking together for some time, Kye and Gillies agreed their interaction as teacher-principal should have shifted from teacher-teacher. Both the men played a part in the breakdown.

After defining the problem, they worked on solutions, talking together for some time, running ideas past each other, incorporating WSpace's impressions that, at times, sent them off in a different direction entirely. Finally, after fine-tuning a last point, Gillies nodded, and Kye murmured "that works for me."

Though there was still work to do, cracks had appeared in their standoff. The impasse was breached. As for WSpace, she was back to her quiet self, and watched the two former friends begin to re-establish some kind of connection.

What they agreed on was Kye could have made his suggestions privately to Gillies. He would not have known everything affecting Gillies' decisions as principal, because Kye wasn't principal. Kye would have just had to live with that inability to know the complete picture, and offer his help if and when it was needed and requested.

For his part, Gillies recognized that his insecurity as principal was Gillies' problem, not that of his staff. He could develop his skills in public speaking, delegation, and collaboration. As well, he could work to delegate, and take advantage of individual strengths of his staff members as assets, not liabilities and threats.

"It's a start," WSpace said to herself, as the three wrapped up the meeting, said their goodbyes, and the drone screen went black.

* * *

It's evening and WSpace, GArea and BSwan are sitting around the table eating leftovers from the night before. GArea and BSwan have their own take on the teacher tension. "It's tough in the heat of your emotions," WSpace sighs, "to back off and give the whole thing some breathing room."

"They should have taken a cue from Anthony Fauci, for godsake," GArea exclaims. Since 1984, Dr. Anthony Fauci was top infectious disease expert to seven American presidents over a career spanning four decades until January 2023. Fauci played a key role at the National Institute of Allergy and Infectious Diseases (NIAID) to develop the AIDS vaccine cocktail. He faced ongoing criticism from AIDS activists who claimed scientists were not moving quickly enough to save lives, and were discriminating against gays, women, and recent immigrants by not including them in their research.[6]

Fauci agreed to meet with the activists. The two sides began to see each other for who they were: concerned, with helpful experience to contribute. One of the activists said the first revealing thing they learned about Fauci's character was his Brooklyn accent. Instead of some anonymous "Elite," his accent told them he was from a working-class neighborhood where, to survive, you learned early to speak plainly, be tough, and not back down.[7]

Fauci played a crucial role in encouraging then U.S. president George W. Bush to dedicate billions of dollars to bring the AIDS cocktail to Africa, where AIDS was killing millions. As Bush told Congress with a wry grin and glint in his eye, "Fauci doesn't come to your office to say 'yes' to something. He's there to tell you what you need to do." Hesitancy on the part of members of Congress turned to support, when Fauci (in Sicilian, Fauci means a "sickle maker") convinced them that African community leaders could make sure Africans took the AIDS cocktail appropriately as prescribed.[8]

Years later, when the COVID19 pandemic struck, Fauci faced a new challenge: to prevent deaths, develop a vaccine, and keep his job under then U.S. president Donald Trump. The two often disagreed on the role of science to fight COVID. Fauci was a target for many who thought COVID was a manufactured hoax.

Politics aside, GArea is impressed with how Fauci handled being in the spotlight. ""He says that, when he's criticized, he tries to not immediately react. That's a really good skill to develop."

BSwan nods, reaching for a chocolate chip cookie from a plate on the table. "Ya, really. If a person lets their feelings get the better of them, reacts, quits and walks away, they've kind of closed the door, right? Oh my god, there's no chance to work for change at all. Zilch. Zip. Nada. Awesome words, huh? Hehe..."

WSpace brings the conversation back to Kye and Gillies. She runs a hand through her hair and yawns, suddenly exhausted, "It's so common. Nobody seemed to know how to solve the situation: Kye and Gillies, school and education officials, nobody." She sat up straighter and tapped her pen with purpose on the table.

"They were all really at a loss, huh," BSwan marvels.

"So much for our education system," GArea guffaws in disgust.

* * *

REVIEW:

1. Do you empathize with Kye or Gillies, or do you empathize with both/neither? Explain.

2. What are WSpace's five steps to come to an agreement? Which do you think is/are most important?

3. Kye and Gillies have what core values in common? What do they differ about?

Over the years, the "point-of-view drone" had dipped and soared around the circle, taking the long view, short view, interpreting actions, motives, blame.

GRAND TOUR

PREVIEW:

1. What does it mean to be a "bridge builder" between people? Explain.

2. Is there a person in your group who is a "bridge builder" between people? If so, who? If not, why not?

* * *

Circles of safety, shifting, breaking, re-forming, like bubbles in a bathtub. Warm. Lukewarm. Cold. Stifling hot.

Obviously, connecting together could benefit everyone. Catch up with each other. Support each person in their journey forward, like linking arms in a united front. That was Tyrone's idea. They'd all been through the same traumatic event. Each experienced it differently, separate points of view like a drone dipping and diving, rising and falling, circling around one unmoving point.

Her death 14 years before. They didn't talk much. Tyrone found it ironic in a time of such easy access to social media. Surely, they just needed to put some effort into it. There was still love there, so much personal history and he was optimistic. The workshop on mending fences had been good. But by the last session, something told him he needed to make it practical face to face. He needed to take an actual "grand tour", so to speak.[1]

Tyrone booked the cheap flights, told friends he was coming their way, and managed to pin down somewhere to stay at each stop. Then he floated the idea to family members that he was "going to be in town." Would they be around, to get together for coffee with him?

The responses were slow coming, like interrupting a freight train moving fast down a track. They were caught up in their own lives, he figured, took note and went ahead.

Her death had been hard for everybody. But they'd moved on, he thought. The families had always been geographically separated. Connection had always taken effort. Various members had tried, to various degrees. Over the years, the "point-of-view drone" had dipped and soared around the circle, taking the long view, short view, interpreting actions, motives, blame.

He went. Various family members met with him. There was joy, tears. (At one point after a long hug, one called out "love you!" as Tyrone was turning to go, and held his glance as Tyrone turned back around.)

It also re-opened wounds. He moved on to the next person. There were painful memories. But there were also steps forward in healing, as he'd hoped. He wasn't able to get together with some people. And others were just plain dismissive.

"They don't need you," said one baldly, face to face, the eyes without emotion and on another occasion, "maybe it's something you did." Another had been kind, but also insinuated some wrongdoing. "Did you ask him to the funeral?"

Yet another responded to Tyrone's overtures in the email subject line: "DO NOT COME HERE." Short, and not sweet. "If you trespass on our property, I will call the police. Get a life."

The grand tour ended with Tyrone visiting the former family home. It felt smaller somehow. But the bones were solid. He looked off in the distance. Echoes of laughter, happiness, sorrow.

"You really can't go home again," Tyrone thought. "Or can you? What does it take? What is it I'm after?"

Mending fences. Fixing what's broken. Keeping them in good shape. Taking on the responsibility, with care and consideration. We talk about mending relationship fences between people. Usually we mean the effort it takes to get along. But a fence also separates. It keeps the divisions and boundaries clear. Tyrone took a last meditative look, started the truck, and headed slowly back down the driveway.

* * *

"You know Tyrone killed the family dog," GArea mutters, taking a sip from his coffee. "What?" Both WSpace and BSwan are startled. WSpace, in the middle of sewing a wayward button back on a shirt, stops mid-stitch, and looks up at GArea.

"Oh, ya." GArea's eyes are wide, triumphant in his inside information. "Killed the family budgies, too." BSwan laughs and sits back, waiting. "The dog thing. Tyrone was late. He rushed out of the house, got into the vehicle. When he backed out of the carport, he drove over the dog who had a habit of lying in the driveway."

Both WSpace and BSwan howl in horror, and look at each other, mouths open in dismay. Instinctively, they cover their eyes with a hand. "Oh my god, and the budgies?" BSwan is biting back laughter.

"Well." GArea is toying with a strand of red licorice. "A young Tyrone - say early 20's - was house-sitting, which involved looking after two budgies in a cage downstairs."

"Go on." WSpace is now also fighting back laughter, the button and shirt set to one side.

"Each day, he'd go down and check on the birds. And each day, they appeared to have plenty of bird seed. He noticed they seemed to be getting more and more friendly, coming up to the bars of their cage, looking at him." WSpace and BSwan are now overcome with emotion, reaching for the tissue box to wipe their eyes.

"Until one day Tyrone went downstairs," GArea pauses for effect.

"And both the budgies were lying immobile on the floor of their cage." WSpace gasps. "They were..." BSwan sighs. "...dead." Silence.

"What Tyrone saw each day were the outer husks of the bird seed." GArea takes a bite of the licorice. "He mistook the empty husks for the bird seed itself."

"Oh," WSpace looks crestfallen. "Why did you tell us this, Gray? What a terrible story."

"In a sense," he takes another bite. "Tyrone made the same mistake with his family. He didn't see, or want to see, what they needed. And there appeared to be no life left in the relationship. At least for him."

PART ONE - FAMOUS OR UNSUNG

"I get it! What was you know a 'circle of safety' wasn't anymore," BSwan chimes in. "He was self-absorbed in his own sort of illusion of what should be. And he didn't see that others might have a different view of the situation."

"So driving over the family dog really showed Tyrone as a 'bull in a china shop', to mix metaphors." WSpace is suddenly solemn, her lips pursed. She pauses for a moment, then starts again. "But I think you're being too hard on him. Tyrone was trying to make something happen, when others weren't." She thinks again. "Maybe they just didn't have the energy."

"Absolutely! He brought some you know fresh energy to the situation," BSwan agrees, "though some may have sort of associated him with a previous trauma, a kind of painful memory they wanted to keep behind them."

"Yes, exactly. Maybe he pushed others too hard," GArea says, "A pull might have been more effective."

"What pull? What else could he do?" WSpace insists heatedly, her eyes pained. "There was very little going on between the families. He was trying to open communication. Some appreciated it."

Over the next hour, the three consider key points of the Tyrone story. They decide that a family "circle of safety" really is fragile. Relationships among any group of people - not just families - are changeable, shifting constantly. A sudden traumatic event can throw everything into chaos, or bring people closer together. Or a bit of both. "Something like that can put pressure on the 'fences' between us." WSpace resumes her sewing.

"'Fences make good neighbors.' It means knowing when to get close to support each other. And when to back off to respect that others are getting on with their lives. Leave it up to them. Set out a 'path of crumbs' to find you, if they want."

"...or bird seed," BSwan grimaces, eyes thoughtful and soft with compassion.

An accident. Ignorance. A lapse in judgment that haunts us for years to come. Getting along means seeing that others are human and make mistakes. They're vulnerable.

Just like us.

* * *

REVIEW:

1. To what extent was Tyrone's idea of a "grand tour" a good or bad idea?

2. What are Tyrone's core values? Explain your choice.

3. What does it mean to be a "bull in a china shop"? How was Tyrone a "bull in a china shop"?

4. Tyrone tried. He could have done better. What does this say about trying in future?

*"How to keep that first joy and excitement?
How to keep the 'us together' attitude?"*

SPORTS, SLAPS, AND FEELING
LIKE A WOMAN

PREVIEW:

1. Are sports all about winning? Explain.

2. Is it ever okay to slap someone? Explain.

3. Apart from cultural expectations, what does it mean to be a man? a woman? Can we know? Explain.

* * *

The drone team is feeling a bit "storied out." So many people in so many different situations trying to get along, at times struggling with conflict. How to make sense of it all? WSpace, GArea and BSwan have no time to lose. The three are hosting an upcoming forum, and have three stories left to explore.

SPORTS RING A DING DING

Team sports and getting along. The drone careened high over one of the inland lakes, the blazing summer sun overhead reflected on its surface. A long narrow object below appeared to crawl. The drone dove towards it and hovered over a dragon boat and its team in full propulsion. Facing the team, the drummer beat a steady rhythm. Twenty paddlers in pairs arched ahead in unison to reach around the person in front. They stabbed their paddle blades to catch below the water, then used leg muscle to haul the boat ahead by pulling back through the water as one. The steersperson from behind stood gripping the long oar, knees cushioning impact, eyes locked ahead gauging the direction of wind and waves.

Technically speaking, for paddlers and rowers "getting along" means moving as one, exactly the same way at exactly the same time (in sync at the same pace). For court, field and rink sports such as basketball, soccer and hockey it means being one crucial piece in a larger puzzle, knowing your role, your part to play, and knowing when to play it, responding to what's going on around you. For court sports like badminton, tennis, pickle ball, it's taking even more responsibility to read your opponent's every move, anticipating and reacting.

Apart from the play itself, team sports all share the same challenge in getting along person to person.

A new sport started in the community. Matt and Talia were curious. They signed up, and were drawn in to the team atmosphere. It was fun, and they were all learning together.

Then, over the years, a split developed between those who were happy to continue as "recreational," and others itching for competition, itching to see how good they could be.

A difference in expectations meant one group fractured into two groups, two cliques.

Talia was good at the sport. She was eager to get better and advance. Matt just enjoyed coming out for the fun, the camaraderie. But it wasn't the same anymore. The competition bug had taken over.

On game days, instead of using the whole team that had signed up at the beginning of the season and practiced together, some players (including Matt) were asked to sit out (particularly those who had missed practices), while "ringers" (skilled players) from other teams took their place.

Talia knew Matt was upset, and she felt sorry for him. At the same time, she said he needed to get better in order to keep up with the team's new direction. That's just the way it was. "We want to win, don't we?" Talia told him. "Isn't that what it's all about?"

* * *

GArea peers over his glasses at his notes and laptop screen. "The sports thing - team sports - are all about competition, winning and losing. That's the nature of the game."

WSpace sees another angle. "Sure. At the same time, team sports are all about group behavior, and that's all about whether players feel they belong or not. There's more to it than just winning and losing."

"It kind of reminds me of the early Beatles," BSwan pipes up. GArea and WSpace look blank. "Okay, together they're becoming a band, you know?

Then the divisions creep in. Half of the band gains a reputation for being great songwriters. Band members are judged as to who is sort of the better musician, superior to the others. How to keep that first joy and excitement? How to keep the 'us together' attitude?" GArea frowns, unimpressed.

"Okay, I get it," WSpace nods. "How to show you value every person's contribution."

"Ya, ya!" BSwan leans towards her.

The use of ringers have them divided. "If you want to win," GArea taps his pen emphatically, "you bring in the best players available."

BSwan counters, "Seriously, what's the point of calling yourself a team if you don't play everyone?"

Sports teams everywhere have their "A team" and "B team": their best and everyone else. Parents argue with coaches over how much "court time" their child gets (court or field, rink, water depending on the sport).

The drone threesome agree that what's key is the team's stated values which need to be clear. To avoid interpersonal tensions, team leaders and coaches need to make decisions based on those values. "If their value is to win at all cost and there may be ringers, then so be it," GArea agrees. "Make sure it's clear to everyone from the beginning of the season. Then everyone knows what to expect, and whether that team is a good fit, or they need to find another kind of team."

* * *

LOOSE SLAP SINKS SMITH

The drone hovered above the glitzy Los Angeles crowd and directly over the agitated actor whose eyes were blazing. Will Smith slapped Chris Rock in the face with an open palm. Then Smith swore at Rock and twice warned Rock to not talk about Smith's wife.

A private personal conversation gone wrong? If only, but no. An estimated 15.36 million people around the world watched in real time as Smith (who later won Best Actor) got violent with Rock (comedian and 2022 Academy Awards co-host). The blow-up shocked viewers and lit up social media for months afterwards.[1]

Clearly Smith was deeply triggered in order to react so strongly. What would cause a well-known figure and role model for kids to lose his composure so completely as the world watched?

Smith, his wife Jada Pinkett Smith and Rock had known each other for years, and worked on separate movies together. In 2023, Pinkett Smith revealed in an autobiography that she and Smith had lived separate lives since 2016, despite public appearances together as a couple.[2]

So, at the 2022 Academy Awards, the "not quite a couple" were sitting in front-row seats in front of the entire audience at the Dolby Theatre in Los Angeles. On the stage a few feet away, Rock was speaking prior to presentation of the award for Best Documentary Feature. He looked at the Smiths and made a "G.I. Jane" joke about Pinkett Smith's shaved head (shaved due to the skin disorder alopecia areata), a reference to the 1997 film starring a shaven Demi Moore.

First, Smith laughed along with the audience, while Pinkett Smith rolled her eyes. Then something in Smith apparently snapped. He got up, walked to Rock on stage, and hit Rock hard. Smith strode back to his seat and screamed at Rock.[3]

Remarks on social media reflected two sides: Smith rightfully defended his wife's honour. (Rock's comment was insensitive and inappropriate.) Smith's violence was unacceptable. (He should have been stripped of his Best Actor award, asked to leave, even charged with assault.)

Smith later resigned from the Academy of Motion Picture Arts and Sciences, and was given a 10-year event ban. A year later, Rock still had not commented widely in public about the incident until a March 2023 Netflix comedy special when Rock insisted he himself was not a victim, but had inadvertently triggered a nerve regarding Smith and Pinkett Smith's own relationship.[4]

* * *

When it came to the Will Smith slap, the drone team collectively shake their heads. This seems to be about feeling humiliation, they think. "The audience was laughing, apparently at his wife's expense," GArea says, leaning back and putting both feet on the chair seat next to him.

"Stand-up comedy lifts public figures and events up to ridicule, and the audience laps it up," GArea is absent-mindedly checking his phone for emails. "But what about when the figures are from your own social circle? And you're making a jab in front of millions of viewers?"

"Seriously," BSwan says, frowning. "People's emotions get triggered by all kinds of things, and we can just lose it, so quickly. But in front of millions at the Academy Awards? When you're up for Best Actor? It's pretty outrageous behavior, ya?"

"Shocked a lot of people that's for sure, maybe even Will Smith himself," WSpace agrees. "It's a good lesson in composure, staying calm and being careful about what you say and do in front of others, hehe, if you can! But I guess that's the point. Sometimes we can't."

* * *

FEELING LIKE A WOMAN

Getting along means understanding each other, or at least understanding where there are gray areas of confusion. One example can be gender. What do we think of when we think "man" or "woman"? The drone shifts back a few years to a British sitting room where two women were talking face to face. The older woman appeared increasingly annoyed.

Germaine Greer, 83, a famous feminist author from the 1970s women's liberation movement, thinks a "woman" is not a pre- or post-operative transgender woman (male to female MTF or M2F).[5]

Core to Greer's thinking is the issue of life experience in all its various forms. In other words, once a man always a man. You can take the genitals and hormones out of the man, but you can't take the male life experience out of a man's head. (The same goes for a woman transitioning to physically become a man.) That isn't to say that a person should not have such a life-altering operation if desired and it's available, Greer insisted. "Carry on, if that's what you think it is you want to do," Greer said in a 2015 BBC Newsnight interview with Kirsty Wark. "I've been accused of inciting violence against transsexual people. That's absolute nonsense." [6]

The whole issue of gender identity and expression is closely tied in with social expectations about looks, physical voice, and behavior. If a man says he "feels like a woman," what is it he's feeling that makes him think "female"? What is it in those feelings that, to him, doesn't fit as a male? Or is there some gender "no man's land" in between? (Think Indigenous Peoples' concept of "two spirits" in one person.)

In the BBC interview, Greer was critical of Glamour magazine awarding its 2015 Woman of the Year award to transgender person Caitlyn Jenner, calling the move "misogynist." [7] For a life-long radical feminist like Greer, the choice of Jenner may trigger a passionate knee-jerk reaction: men again taking the rightful spotlight away from women.

* * *

The drone threesome take a break. When they sit back down, it's BSwan who takes the lead and launches into an explanation of gender choice.

Afterwards GArea glares at BSwan. "What the hell are you talking about?"

"Watch your language, Gray, we're recording," WSpace says calmly.

"Well, Swan can watch Swan's language, for godsake! I'm trying to understand this whole gender thing, and talking in 'gender speak' jargon doesn't help."

BSwan had begun the conversation by presenting a transgender point of view.

"You know, thinking there's a 'real woman' is negative essentialism," BSwan had started. "And it's false to think that we can't know the opposite end of the intersex spectrum so we can't know that we have a different gender identity. Many transgender folk and others in the 2SLGBTQI+ community sort of think this is transphobia and uses gender stereotypes, okay?" [8]

After GArea's outburst, BSwan is eyeing the older man warily through long locks of hair. "We talk this way because it's a sort of shortcut for the kind of gender diversity we're seeing nowadays, alright? Sorry if you're confused. Think of it this way: like when someone speaks another language, do you blame them? No, like you get busy and learn the language. But I see what you mean."

"Do you?" GArea has calmed down slightly. "If you want me to understand, it really helps to talk in plain language. Sure, I'll try to pick up some of these gender words, okay?"

PART ONE - FAMOUS OR UNSUNG   87

"Okay, so I'll start again," BSwan pushes the hair to one side. "So do you understand what 2SLGBTQI+ means?"

"I think so," GArea sits up straighter. "Lesbian, gay, bisexual, trans-gender, queer, two spirit... What's the 'I'?"

"Awesome. The 'I' is 'intersex,' like not the typical biological sex differences.[9] So, the 2SLGBTQI+ community kind of thinks that it's murky to try to define 'man' or 'woman.' If you think of gender as a spectrum," BSwan's hands are up, far left and far right, "much of the whole point of the gender scene in society right now is exploration."

BSwan leans in, eyes wide, looking to confirm GArea is following. GArea nods listening.

"The 'Q' in 2SLGBTQI+ also means folk who are questioning. It's all about feelings. What feels right, true, authentic? It's kind of exploring identity along that spectrum and even outside the spectrum, ya? Pushing boundaries.

"Okay, so transgender folk have sort of changed their bodies to the other gender: male to female (MTF or M2F), or female to male (FTM or F2M). Or maybe not. Maybe they've still got their original genitals. The big thing is they feel like they're the other gender, and they want people to see them as the other gender, right? They feel they belong there. Greer doesn't want to sort of give them that, okay, so they think she's stifling them and she's got a 'phobia' about trans folk."

BSwan pauses, then suddenly says, "And remember the history of bullying and violence against 2SLGBTQI+ folk, even laws against homosexuality. Oh my god, some people even thought same-sex attraction was a mental illness." BSwan also pointed to 2015 statistics that suicide rates were eight times higher among transgender young people than their 18- to 24-year-old peers, and that crimes against transgender people were on the rise.[10]

"You're not transgender, right?" GArea is settling into a contemplative curiosity. "No," BSwan says. "I'm non-binary." GArea looks blank. "That means I don't you know think of myself as strictly male or female. It's pretty open." GArea nods.

"Some transgender can't explain why they feel the way they do," BSwan continues patiently. "They just know that it's really uncomfortable, really torture, traumatic, to live life as their birth gender. What they see in the mirror isn't what they feel inside.[11]

"You know, whether they do the operation or not, it's not easy to make the jump, okay? It's not like they wake up one morning and say 'I think I'll be that other gender,' you know? And it's very sort of personal. It's not about making things complicated for that other gender; there's lots of respect. The attitude is kind of like 'hey, there's gender room enough for both of us.'

"Oh ya, and one more thing. Trans-gender people say they should have the same access to their chosen gender's spaces and rights, okay? They say people in general treat them like their chosen gender, because the trans-gender person presents themselves as their chosen gender. It's not just about clothes, names."[12]

"Does that help?" BSwan turns to GArea. "Ya, that helps a lot."

"Awesome!" BSwan adds, "Ya, at the same time some young feminists in particular can, you know, go a bit overboard in being intersectional."

"Huh?" GArea's mouth is open.

"That means being sensitive to race, class, disability, sexualities and identities," BSwan says.[13] "Don't get me wrong, that's a really good thing. They like to let these folk speak for themselves, which is cool. But to, say, totally slam Greer and want to ban her from talking publicly, one of the most significant living feminists? [14] Seriously, even if she's a TERF, she must have *something* good to say."

"What?" GArea leans forward.

"Oh, that's 'trans-exclusionary radical feminist.' A bad thing," [15] BSwan says sighing. "You want to be a TGIF: a 'transgender inclusive feminist.'"

"Nothing to do with Fridays?" "No."

WSpace had been taking the whole conversation in, listening.

"The whole issue today of gender identity, orientation, expression is so divisive maybe because it's so misunderstood," she says. "It triggers different life experiences. Greer sees cisgender women being pushed to the side as usual. But the young feminists are triggered by the needs of other folk who've historically been pushed to the side."

"Cisgender?" GArea is on it in a flash.

"Yes, it means when you're comfortable with the gender you were born with," WSpace turns to him.

"I can't help but think of the stories of transgender female bodybuilders, say, who win medals in women's categories," WSpace continues musing.

"Their bodies are different, and the cisgender women can't compete with them. And then there's the issue of transgender access to women's public spaces. You hear about men posing as transgender women to get into a women's public toilet, pedophiles even. It's all just so complicated.

"I can't help but wonder what a transgender person is identifying with when they feel like a 'woman'? Just asking, you know. I want to understand, too. We grow up with such limited media images and expectations of what men and women are. It's tragic! I'm thinking that human beings are a whole lot more than padded bras, high heels and makeup."

GArea's eyes are twinkling. "Men, too?" WSpace laughs. "Of course!"

"Seriously, it's what we've been talking about all along," BSwan is ready to move on. "You know listening to each other. Sort of being curious about the other's experiences. We don't get anywhere if we're not willing to sit down together and kind of talk about it."

"Got it! Thanks Swan, you big guy," GArea reaches over, gives BSwan a bear hug and ruffles Swan's hair. "I mean big They/Them!" BSwan looks sheepish but pleased, and reaches quickly to mess GArea's hair. "Hey!" GArea barks with a hearty laugh. "Watch the bald spot! I'm growing veggies up there!"

* * *

REVIEW:

1. What do you think about the use of "ringers" in sports?

2. To what extent did the Academy of Motion Picture Arts and Sciences do the right thing, after Will Smith hit Chris Rock?

3. To what extent do you think Germaine Greer should be banned from speaking publicly?

4. In each of these three stories, what are the core values? Explain your choices.

PART TWO -
Mind, Emotion & Spirit

"Everything we'll be talking about today is kind of in flux. Like, nothing is set in stone. You know, we're all here to learn."

"TIP TALK" FORUM

PREVIEW:

1. When a lot of people have a lot of things to say, what's one good way of organizing the gathering? Explain.

* * *

WSpace, GArea and BSwan have finished discussing the stories. It's time to bring in other people interested in the topic of conflict resolution, speakers from all walks of life. There is a buzz of excitement in the virtual air.

"Thank you for joining us this morning," WSpace addresses the crowd of participant faces on the call conference screen, a complete wall of the drone work room to one side of the front windshield. The drone rests in a forest clearing, and the hum is barely audible. Out the windshield, the first glimpse of a brilliant orange sun is just visible rising over a hillside in the distance.

"You're each familiar with the stories GArea, BSwan and I have been studying." Heads nod. WSpace pauses looking down at her papers, and grits her teeth behind closed lips. "We've had a slight change of plans. Because we're under such a tight deadline, we've had to limit each presentation to five minutes each."

Group audio is turned off, but heads jerk up, and eyes and mouths widen. Then several of the participants scramble to make adjustments, heads bent over notes and electronics. "We apologize," WSpace adds brightly, "and we also have confidence that you will present your most important findings. We'll record for future study."

To each side of WSpace at the table, her colleagues GArea and BSwan (both in their best available shirts, hair combed) sit with hands clasped. They silently survey the rows of participant faces. WSpace turns to BSwan, who takes a breath. "Ya! We're calling this forum 'TIP Talk,'" BSwan says.

"'TIP' for 'Tips In Progress.' Everything we'll be talking about today is kind of in flux. Like, nothing is set in stone. You know, we're all here to learn."

GArea nods. "You can use your five minutes to comment directly on one or more of the stories, or what another presenter has said. Or you can use your time to get into some theory, some practice, etcetera, etcetera." He waves a hand. "Also," BSwan continues, "if you really need more time, you can claim your 'TIP Talk green card' okay, which will give you another five minutes, but no more, ya?"

"So," WSpace adjusts her chair, "thank you for bringing your expertise today. It will be fascinating."

"And practical." GArea leans in, looking pointedly at each presenter in turn.

BSwan reaches for a chart. "Ya, we've given you each a random number to keep things simple. Okay, then. First up is One."

At Number 10, people are losing interest. Some of the other presenters are stifling yawns, leaning on an elbow, looking down and discretely closing their eyes.

"Can I suggest something?" rasps a large woman in her 60's in a brightly flowered dress, after Number 10 has wrapped up his talk. "This is all just bits and pieces. We need to combine them together somehow."

"I agree," says a diminutive woman in her 30's, long straight black hair partially concealing her eyes. "Can we listen to everyone, then get together in groups to make final group presentations?"

"Ya, ya." The raspy woman is nodding her head vigorously. "We can get together in break-out rooms." As they are talking, a trans-gender person typing furiously asks to co-host for a minute, then shows the group a chart. "Here's my GANTT chart template.[1] How about we listen and rate each presenter 1-5 according to how well we think our stuff meshes with theirs. Maybe limit groups to five people or so. Then consider the top four other presenters to group with?"

Nods of approval, thumbs up, and other reaction emojis light up the wall. Now they would have something to focus their attention while they're listening. Some start typing. Others write in notebooks, or talk into phones. Still others are speaking into phones and recording. WSpace, GArea and BSwan lean in to each other, consider the chart, and whisper together.

"Great idea," GArea is peering over glasses. "We'll be tight on time, but your ideas will make for a better forum, and stronger submissions. Thank you for this! We'll finish the individual presentations today. Please listen for the other four you want to work with. And include alternates."

"This evening, WSpace, BSwan and I will go over your choices and make break-out room lists for tomorrow. Your group will need to have a presentation paper or recording done and in to us by the end of the following day." A flurry of activity turns the drone wall into a whir of motion. Some presenters are already sending chats to others to line up groups. "Alright then! Let's have a 10-minute break then get back at it. Next breaks are lunch, afternoon coffee, and dinner. We'll aim to finish at seven."

"Presenter 11? Ready to go?" By 7 p.m., everyone looks exhausted, their heads full of the day's information. They agree to split the research topics into three broad categories that WSpace, GArea and BSwan will separate the breakout-room groups into: Mind, Emotion and Spirit.

With a final wave, one by one the participant screens go black. BSwan makes hot chocolate, buttered toast, and fills a bowl with nuts and apples. Together the drone threesome get to work.

* * *

REVIEW:

1. How do WSpace, GArea and BSwan decide to organize the 'TIP Talk' Forum? Who has ideas?

CHAPTER ONE -
Mind

"It's that back and forth with each other that sets us up for survival."

FLOWERED DRESS: CAN I TRUST YOU?

PREVIEW:

1. What does "trust" mean to you?
2. What's the difference between having a conversation, and having a debate?
3. What does group support have to do with mental health?

* * *

The raspy-voiced woman in the flowered dress is the presenter for the first group. The clock is ticking so she wastes no time in pulling out a bright red apple and taking a large bite. As she munches, the screen crowd looks confused. FDress swallows, takes a sip of water, and begins.

"Calling an Indigenous person an 'apple' – red on the outside and white on the inside – is very derogatory, a real insult. No one wants to be accused of not sharing the group's values or being disloyal.[1]

"As human beings, all of us have a very deep need to belong, to trust others and build a name, a reputation for being trustworthy," FDress says. "Without a group that supports us and believes in us, we feel vulnerable. At the same time, every day we're all pushing the boundaries of our groups because every person in the group has a different point of view. That's what I'm going to talk about."[2]

Take Chief Clarence Louie, for example, FDress begins. He straddles two worlds, courting the modern business world to improve the living standard of his Indigenous community. The overlap between the two groups is the entrepreneurial spirit that has marked North American Indigenous Peoples for millennia. What allows Louie to straddle the two worlds successfully is that his group clearly benefits. A common value is providing needed jobs and services.

"Can't get others to get along?" she asks the screen audience. "Often it's like herding cats: people with different ways of thinking going off in all directions. Former U.S. president Jimmy Carter was very conscious of that!"

Throughout his public life, Carter went into high-stakes mediation with intention that set a tone: others saw he was there to listen and understand, so they tended to trust him. Carter, Egyptian President Anwar Sadat, and Israeli Prime Minister Menachem Begin met in 1978 for the Camp David peace talks. It was the last day, and talks were stalled. Carter was ready to return to Washington, D.C. in failure. Prime Minister Begin asked Carter if he would sign a photo of the three world leaders for each of Begin's eight grandchildren. Carter's secretary Susan Clow phoned to Israel for the grandchildren's names. Carter personally autographed a photo for each child by name: "With love and best wishes to [name] from Jimmy Carter, [with Carter's signature]." When Carter presented the photos to Begin, the Israeli Prime Minister was moved to tears by the gesture, and Carter had tears, too. After the leaders' previous efforts at a resolution, Prime Minister Begin had been angry. But the anger immediately changed. What may have looked to some like an unimportant sentimental detail helped shift the peace talks. Begin offered to stay and try again, and an agreement was eventually reached.[3]

"Treating the other person as a human being with feelings and emotions (and grandchildren they love dearly) does matter. It's important to take personal responsibility to treat them that way," FDress stresses. "Okay, so what I'm going to talk about next is alliance-building, gathering allies."

Nothing happens between people unless there's trust, she begins. To get something happening, you need to interact, connect, and build rapport. How to do that? Key is to be open, honest and transparent with your motives, the interests behind your actions. Listen to others and aim to understand. Assume good intent. Ask for clarification: "Are you saying this, or this?" Don't debate. Have a conversation. Be curious. Where do your goals overlap? See the other person as a partner, not an enemy.[4]

After Carter left office, he and his wife Rosalynn Carter started the Carter Center with a mission to have: "the courage to break new ground, fill vacuums, and address the most difficult problems in the most difficult situations," and it "recognizes that solving difficult problems requires careful analysis, relentless persistence, and the recognition that failure is an acceptable risk." [5]

When working internationally with feuding world leaders, Carter had a simple technique. He would meet with one leader, and take lots of notes. Then he'd go back to his room and write (or type) his notes. He'd do the same with the next leader involved in the dispute.

Afterwards, based on these notes, Carter would put possible points of agreement on one piece of paper. He would put this document into his pocket as a focus for the next set of talks. Again, Carter would listen to each leader's reactions and suggestions, then go back and forth between the separate rooms. Carter gave each leader mental space, and stayed curious. He rewrote his document as many as two dozen times.[6]

FDress delves more deeply. "Some social scientists say that humans as social primates evolved for maximum interaction. It's that back and forth with each other that sets us up for survival. None of us has the full picture of what is real. But when each person shares their point of view, the whole group gets a more full, broad perspective." FDress coughs, takes a drink of water, and leans forward in her chair closer to the screen. She speaks more quickly, and waves a hand to emphasize her point, visibly excited. "The trick is that to take full advantage, the rest of the group needs to listen deeply. Scientists think disagreement, even argument, is socially useful, even necessary. One person presents a viewpoint. The others give pros and cons. Together they hash it out, collaborate, and get stronger as a group than by themselves."[7]

"So how do we do that well?" FDress pauses for effect. "Share your point clearly. Educate the others. Help the others to think more deeply about why they think what they do. Focus on their reasoning, their motivation. What have any of you missed?" [8]

"You make it sound so easy," WSpace smiles softly, meeting FDress' eye. "Well, in a sense it is," FDress replies, shrugging her shoulders and raising her hands and eyebrows. "It's all about giving the other person emotional space to tell their story and unpack their past experience. It's emotional reasoning, and it's where the gold is. If you dig deeply enough, people may reveal why they think what they think." [9]

That's alliance-building. But to connect with others *outside* the group, it's important to know you're welcome *inside your own* group. "If we don't have a solid community that supports us," FDress reiterates, "if we don't have a role in the group, we're vulnerable to jealousy, shame, embarrassment. We care a lot about what others think of us, and we're extremely sensitive to the differences that set groups apart. What's really disturbing is we'd rather have our own small group look good, than worry about what's good for the larger community. We'd rather be accepted than be right." [10]

Don't take your group for granted. You go to your group for rest, sustenance and to recharge. Your group can help you be resilient, adapt and grow, to rebuild purpose and meaning in life. On the other hand, a group can also judge and control. Think cults and extremism.

FDress pauses, looks down at her notes, then looks solemnly into the camera's lens. "Think for a moment about someone who's suicidal. What could be happening? How are they doing in their group? Do they even have a group? How does that person feel about the group? How in tune is that person with their own feelings? Are they having trouble understanding their own feelings?

"What about that suicidal person and trust, reputation? There are all kinds of group signs of loyalty around clothes, music, cars, attitudes, beliefs, stated opinions. Jobs, careers, amount of money you have. In a group, these things can be a sign of loyalty or shame. If your values are different from the group, you might get a bad reputation, be labelled as an outsider and less than trustworthy. It can lead to serious emotional harm.[11]

"If we can't trust people in our group," FDress adds, "we'll argue to try to fix the problem. If we can't fix it, we may be looking for another group that accepts us and will take us in."

"The brain is amazing." FDress is coming to the end of her talk. "It's always looking for patterns so it knows what to expect. When something wild and crazy happens (or even just a period of upheaval), a person's brain sorts through that person's life experiences to explain it. The brain wants to rationalize and justify. Disagreements happen because the brain of each person involved is doing the same thing, but with different life experiences. Nothing is objective, and evidence can seem irrelevant." How to work with this flurry of brain activity? Slow things down, FDress says, and make talking together safe. If we feel safe, we might ask ourselves to what extent our past experience is outdated. Do I need to update my perspective? "That takes courage to admit," FDress stresses. "What's working? What's not? 'Maybe I'm wrong here.'" You may have different positions, but similar interests. A good question to also ask is "Why do we see things differently?" [12]

"Think about all the parts of the world in these stories," FDress raises her arms wide. "What's culture? It's people with different viewpoints coming together to compare how they see things, and bringing together all their separate views." [13]

"What if there's a crisis, and everything's in chaos?" a man from the viewing audience is unmuted so he can ask. "The person has massive change coming at them from all sides. Won't the reaction be to close up, to cling even tighter to that person's positions?"

"Good point," FDress responds. "Once the evidence is overwhelmingly against them and they can't ignore it anymore, they change. It can be pretty traumatic. Think Indigenous Peoples and first contact with Europeans. What had been reality isn't reality anymore. People change when they need to, and that takes courage. Sometimes change is like a drop of water wearing away stone. Sometimes it's very sudden and unexpected." [14]

BSwan is pointing to a timer. FDress sees it out of the corner of her eye. She ends her presentation. "Wherever you go in the world, people are asking themselves 'who can I trust?' That's a very human question."

* * *

REVIEW:

1. Regarding human viewpoints, how is "culture" created?

2. Give two examples of how former U.S. President Jimmy Carter helped world leaders get along.

3. Disagreeing can be useful. How?

4. What are the core values of FDress' talk? Explain your choice.

"A good dialogue can have the loose nature of a conversation; the focused approach to learning of training; or the heated passion, vigor, and even anger of a debate. . . While the dialogues were able to bridge race lines, we had greater challenges in crossing class and education lines." [1]
-Lisa Schirch & David Campt

SILKY: YOUTH MEETS AGE-OLD WISDOM

PREVIEW:

1. Several people are arguing together. How do you handle the situation?
2. Where does anger come from? Explain.

* * *

The on-line gallery of dozens of tiny box screens is lighting up one by one after a short toilet break. The next speaker is a young woman with long silky straight black hair parted in the middle and curtaining either side of her large eyes. Behind her on a wall are posters of an internationally famous Kazakhstan singing sensation, a seven-person Korean boy band who'd taken the world by storm, and a popular young Swedish environmental activist yelling passionately to a massive crowd.

Silky's hair covers much of her face, and falls below her shoulders. She silently studies her screen notes, as WSpace introduces the second in the "Mind" presentations.

GArea is studying the woman. "She doesn't look much older than 18," he thinks to himself, "fresh out of high school. This oughta be interesting."

"For sure," BSwan murmurs, texting on a phone. GArea turns sharply, gaping. What?

The room and screens go quiet. The young woman glances up, catches the nod from WSpace, and begins with a Scottish toast: "May the roof above never fall in, and may we below never fall out."[2]

"In life, we're going to 'fall out' with other people," Silky begins with authority in her voice. "At times, life is full of tension and conflict. We saw with the Himalayan villagers, the grandfather comment, that education can divide a group. There's judgment. It can be quite tough to get people of different education levels to talk comfortably together."

"The best we can hope for is 'ubuntu'." Silky pauses, and looks directly at the camera. Some forum participants nod in understanding. Others look puzzled. She explains that the African Zulu word means the spirit of connection, community, belonging. At core, with all our diversity, we're still one human race. A person who values "ubuntu" is solid in themselves, and behaves that way. They feel they belong, don't feel threatened, and are sensitive to the feelings of others.[3]

"Ya. Let's take another look at the story of educators Kye and Gillies, and how they you know showed ubuntu or not," she says. "How did these two educated, intelligent men who had been friends get into this situation of being adversaries? And how could they have kind of gotten themselves out?"

"The best they were able to do at the time was Gillies as principal met with Kye. Both were upset. Behind the scenes, an education official talked with both of them separately. Wow, really? There was no goal to the meetings made clear at the beginning, no set of collaborative values that could have guided them as they tried to talk to each other, no set purpose," Silky pauses. "Oh my god! Basically it was two agitated people expected to work things out on their own, with one of them having official power over the other. Seriously! How well is that going to work?" Though the crowd is muted, several people smile and chuckle. They can relate. It generally doesn't work well.

"Though there will always be tensions and conflicts, there is a way to deal with it." Silky turns a page, her eyes directed at the webcam, jaw set. Across the screens, participants, GArea, BSwan and WSpace reach for keyboards, pen and paper as Silky continues.

There once was a man named Rumi (Silky begins as if reading a fairy tale to a child) who was excited about bringing the Indigenous circle process to his group. But when he explained the role of the "talking piece" (an eagle feather) to the other nine people, six said outright they didn't want to do it. They didn't want to take "three hours." One outspoken critic said outright she "didn't need an eagle feather" to make a decision.

Also, the Critic was apparently okay with taking over discussions, and cutting in whenever an idea occurred to her. Another six men and women responded or not to her outbursts. Rumi was largely shunted to the side of the conversation, as were three of the quieter members.

These other three, and Rumi, used the eagle feather to show they had something to say, but were often ignored. Rumi felt ridiculous. As a discussion tool, the talking piece is supposed to guide the whole group. Ideally, it has a calming effect. (Everyone has an opportunity to talk, as well as listen.) But Rumi felt himself getting anxious, becoming tongue-tied, as he listened to the others who spoke more quickly than he did.

After they left, he felt totally deflated, sitting dejectedly in one corner, going over in his mind what had happened. What went wrong? He really felt his own dignity had been undermined. He hadn't been shown respect. During the meeting, he felt himself getting upset, angry, withdrawing.

When he had tried to point out how the others were talking over each other, the Critic's emotions were immediately triggered into reaction. She got angry, said she didn't have to be there and had better things to do, and could walk out the door. Over the following months, Rumi noticed a pattern. The Critic would often do the same thing whenever she strongly disagreed. At one point she said it was her fiery "Irish blood." But Rumi saw it as more of a useful habit that the Critic learned would often shut others down and get the Critic her way. Why change?

At this particular meeting, the others were silent as she ranted. Rumi said nothing, waiting. After the Critic's vent, the Critic exhaled deeply. She had gotten the space she needed, or at least wanted. Now she might be ready to listen to others. So Rumi did learn something from the meeting. Don't rise to another person's emotion. See it out; control your own reaction. Silence is powerful.

Later thinking back, Rumi could see other clues to what had gone wrong. The Critic had come to the meeting already in a shell-shocked frame of mind, from an incident at home earlier that day. Her email account had been hacked. After the meeting at Rumi's, the Critic returned to deliver something they'd talked about. Alone with her, Rumi took the opportunity to tell her that he hadn't liked "fast-thinkers/ fast-talkers" talking over "slow-thinkers/ slow-talkers." He looked her in the eye, and said he hoped they could "compromise." The Critic seemed taken aback, and said nothing.

As the Critic turned to leave, Rumi called out that it had been a difficult morning for her. Pure gold. He acknowledged that the hacked account at home that morning had shaken the Critic's very human need for safety and security. Rumi was showing he understood and had empathy.

In an earlier meeting, the Critic had been somewhat sarcastic, cynical. She talked about how she disliked "kumbaya" thinking, as if she sensed it on the horizon. In fact, the word "kumbaya" ("come by here") comes from the American South, and an Afro-American spiritual song called "Oh Lord, Won't You Come By Here." The song is about unity, peace, harmony, goodness. Some people think the idea that you can talk together to arrive at solutions is childish, naive, idealistic, and out of touch with the real world. They think dialogue is passive and a distraction, not effective space for creativity. It's just not practical.[4]

Rumi knew what he had to do. He needed to show the others that it's not for nothing the Indigenous circle process and talking piece have helped resolve conflict around the world for thousands of years. That's because it works.

He decided the next meeting would be different. He would set a meeting time deadline and, with the group, come up with a list of core values as guidelines going forward for the rest of the year. Values such as prudent use of time, focus on facts, trust, respect, listening. What would be expected of one group member, would be expected of all. They could maybe take a cue from the Rotary International service club's Four-Way Test: 1. Is it true? (What is truth? Personal experience? Evidence? Both?) 2. Is it fair to all? 3. Does it build good will and better friendships? 4. Is it beneficial to all concerned? [5]

Rumi would address group concerns one by one. He didn't want to get tough. (Taking a "power over" approach doesn't make for long-term relationships.) But he would insist that together they try dialogue using a talking piece, any talking piece. He would cut his explanations to the bare minimum. (It's use of the talking piece - not the chairperson - that regulates a meeting conversation.) As group members, they were all responsible for getting along.

It sounded good on paper. But when the time came at the next meeting, he realized the talking piece idea wouldn't work "with this group at this time." He told them so. They sat in silence, listening to him be flexible. He told himself he would do his best to help them through a challenging time of transition. He would show - at their meetings, and at other times - that he was realistic, practical, trustworthy, and respectful. He was someone who valued his own time, as well as that of others. He could handle the gritty challenges of the real world - talking piece in mind, if not in hand.

Silky brings the drone forum participants back to the present. "What I like about the Rumi story," she says, "is it shows that, though it's not always easy to work with others who have a different viewpoint, it can be done. Ya! What's the lesson? Persevere, okay? Go slow to go fast. Open up. Listen to criticism, and learn."

In the case of the two educators Kye and Gillies, she says, they have different beliefs and values, based on different life experiences. They had worked together quite well, until they saw a threat to values. There was also a clash of influences coming from other people, perceptions of the situation, and fears of consequences. Kye and Gillies both had a piece of the truth. They needed to put their pieces together.[6]

Silky goes to screen share, with some checklists. Several of the participants reach for their phones to take photos. "Think of emotional triggers as sticks of dynamite taped to our past experiences, ready to blow. Like BOOM!" Silky's eyes are wild and wide. She throws her hands high in the air. The forum participants laugh. Then she pulls herself together, and calmly puts the first table up on the screen. "We may have no idea what will trigger someone else's feelings into reaction. So how do we deal with it?" *(see trigger checklist)*.

"That's where the circle process comes in, okay?" Silky reaches for the next screen table *(see Indigenous circle process checklist)*. "Indigenous Peoples around the world use it, oceans apart. Awesome, I know!"

"In this circle thing these sets of questions can help focus a group, to keep people from going off in all directions. Keep in mind though," she adds, "that what looks chaotic may just be creative thinking before a group decides what they can live with." [7]

"Ya! And remember: if you aren't getting anywhere with someone, it can be really helpful to stop and ask them if you sort of understand their feelings and needs. Go back and forth with them for a while to clarify, you know, maybe in private." [8]

Silky stops. Her face softens into a shy smile. She pushes each panel of hair back behind her ears, and thanks participants for listening. They erupt into emoji claps, smiles, and thumbs up.

"Thank you!" WSpace is smiling broadly. "And please thank the rest of your project group for a very informative and thought-provoking presentation!" WSpace turns to GArea and BSwan. "I think we can all agree that it's tough when someone in a group - or even the group itself – isn't understanding each other, 'doesn't want to dance,' so to speak." Heads are nodding. "I love to dance," GArea quips, swiveling his hips. WSpace laughs then says, "We're going to break for lunch, and be back in an hour for our next presentation."

* * *

REVIEW:

1. What does "ubuntu" mean? What does "kumbaya" mean?

2. Why didn't Rumi's group want to use a talking piece?

3. What are the core values of Silky's talk? Explain your choice.

TRIGGER: What Makes Me Tick (like a time bomb)? (lessons from Restorative Justice) [9]
T= TENSION (Loss of trust? Someone in my space?)
R= 'RE-RUN' RESPONSE (Am I remembering a painful memory from the past?)
I= IMPRESSION (Is there an imbalance between interests? Take the initiative to connect.)
G= GOALS (Focus on creating guidelines.)
G= GROUP GOODWILL (Get to the bottom of the problem.)
E= EXPERIENCES (Explore emotions. Explain. Is there equity? Is there a gap in social class, and education level?)
R= RE-SET (Recognize with respect what you have in common.)

PART TWO - MIND, EMOTION & SPIRIT

INDIGENOUS CIRCLE PROCESS [10]
HISTORY= Influenced Maslow's Hierarchy of Needs
IDEA= Face each other in a circle; talk & listen Pass the talking piece consecutively (every time to the right, or every time to the left): 1) share my thoughts? 2) be silent? OR 3) pass it on? What can you agree with?
BELIEFS/VALUES= dignity; respect; relationship collaborate; show my best self; connect
FOCUS= Individual experience; stories; needs of all; balance (NOT= finding fault; punishment)
PARTS= 1) *Circle Keeper* (calm; helps set guidelines; makes safe space) 2) *Talking Piece* (symbolic of respect; passed in consecutive order; regulates talking)

RELATIONSHIP IN ACTION [11]
YES = -Accept others as they are with dignity; address needs -Support the wellbeing of others; engage (don't judge); be positive
YOU = -Clarify; give specifics; define for understanding -Be fair and just; work through the discomfort -Goal: healthy relations; healing
CAN = -Share power; match expectations with support

CHECKLIST TO CONFRONT CONFLICT: [12]

1. What happened, is happening?
2. What's the cause? (What's my role? Did I harm or exclude someone else?)
3. What was/am I feeling and thinking about it? (I didn't think it was a problem, but they're really triggered?)
4. What is the hardest (best) thing about it for me?
5. Who is affected by this? How? What are the harms, needs? Who has a stake in the situation? Include everyone involved. What matters to the person? (Listen harder when you disagree.)
6. What do I and others need to do to move forward? Who's obligated to help? Ask for feedback first. Be practical (scarcity is constant). Don't wait for the perfect moment. Anytime is ripe for peace-building. Share my own experience, learning, objections.
7. Include the person who did the harm, so they can rise above the harm done, make things right, and feel that they are "a good person." (Taking responsibility to make amends is more effective in the long-run than punishment.)
8. What's the stumbling block?
9. How to get beyond it? (use core values)
10. Recognize common ground.
11. Evaluate success. (How well did this process work?)
12. When you disagree, say this: "excuse me" (slow the conversation); "so what you're saying is" (try to understand); find out what matters to the person (listen harder when you disagree); share your own experience, learning, objections.

CHAPTER TWO -
Emotion

"It's also important to prepare for meetings and hard conversations," John stresses. "Don't just go in 'cold turkey.' What! Are you an amateur?? Make notes and go over them, even role-play with a partner. Thinking you can just wing it doesn't fly."

LEADERSHIP AND COURAGE:
THE EMOTIONAL CLIFF

PREVIEW:

1. What do feelings and emotions have to do with getting along with others in a group?
2. What is "courage"? Describe a time when you saw courage in action, and/or you had courage.

* * *

Everything about him speaks no-nonsense "military." From the drone's wall screen, he sits impassive, a chiseled face, buzz-cut hair, lean ebony muscular arms gleaming from under his short-sleeved khaki T-shirt, a stark overhead light throwing shadows across the bare steel table, water glass, pen, and white stack of notes.

The room and on-line participants are silent. Colonel John wastes no time, his voice a deep, rich baritone that sends the drone's speaker system bass tones reverberating. Listeners scramble to adjust their speakers. "I'm not here to talk empty ideas and philosophy. I'm here to tell you what I've seen on the ground in the military about leadership and courage."

"It may not be what you expect."

John glances down at his notes, reaches for a pair of dark-framed glasses, and settles in. "Courage means putting yourself on the line, taking a calculated risk. You have no guarantee things will work out as planned. You can't see what's to come. That makes you very vulnerable."

"To do something courageous, you need to know who you are, and you need to know who the people you're dealing with are. What makes you all tick as people? I'm going to give you a toolkit. Call it 'Twelve Tools to Build Courage 101.'" After saying this, Colonel John has a story to tell.

* * *

COURAGE 1: BUILD THEIR CONFIDENCE AND SHARE DECISION-MAKING [1]

"Genghis Khan apparently knew how to 'find the leader' in the talented people around him, and take advantage of their potential," Colonel John begins. "Genghis Khan delegated leadership of his conquered lands to his daughters, and monitored their progress. They did well. Not every leader is born with that ability to spread the leadership around. But it can be learned."

For example, former U.S. Navy Captain L. David Marquet completely changed the way he led, Colonel John says. In 1999, Marquet took over command of the U.S. nuclear submarine USS Santa Fe. "It was really struggling," John says. "The Santa Fe was worst in the fleet in morale, performance, and the number of crew members who quit (retention rate)."

After Marquet realized his crew knew more about this particular sub than he did, he started consulting with them more, John explains. Marquet clearly expressed his goals and objectives, and made sure his crew had all the training they needed. Then Marquet told his crew he expected them to come up with solutions to the problems and issues they were bringing to him. Crew members became more assertive. Morale jumped dramatically, as did performance. Santa Fe rose to the top in the fleet. Crew members stayed. Several went on to command other submarines.

"What Marquet did might not work in every situation," John adds. "A different group may have different backgrounds, and not want to work independently and take responsibility. They may not like this kind of approach, and say 'that's not the way we do things here'.

"The kind of changes Marquet saw in crew attitude didn't happen overnight," John stresses. "It takes a lot of patience from the person in charge. It's a long-term focus. You'll need fortitude, strength and stamina. Can you handle the setbacks?"

When it works, it's extremely powerful. You're freeing group members to express what they already know. Once you tell them the goals, they decide what needs to be done and how. You help them when and how you can to reach their personal goals.

COURAGE 2: CLARIFY INTENTIONS AND EXPECTATIONS [2]

"Things fall apart when we feel we don't belong," John stresses. "Maybe the 'ground rules' for the group are unclear. Then we tend to close up to protect ourselves, get secretive, go on the attack. When we think of the Himalayan villagers, their group 'ground rules' are clear. The Mosuo, same thing (though the modern world is pushing in)."

The Critic vented on Rumi, going on the attack and using the "talking stick" group leader as a punching bag. It takes courage to hunt for clarity, to ask tough questions, to "pin" people down about what they mean by their words and behavior (not "put" them down). Is the time right to do so?

"But stealth intentions and expectations are dangerous, and they're everywhere," John says. Stealth means being cautious, calculating, secretive. (A "stealth" bomber, for example, can't be detected by the latest anti-aircraft technology.) We do it to try to protect ourselves.

"For example, it seems the situation between Jody Wilson-Raybould and the PMO, and educators Kye and Gillies had stealth intentions and expectations that caused damage," John suggests. "It seems they all really needed a dose of clarity."

COURAGE 3: FEELINGS RULE [3]

"The fact of the matter is that feelings rule," John says. "You want to do two things. Ask yourself how feelings are ruling you: needs, drivers, triggers. Your fears, anxiety. All that. And what about your group's feelings? Be honest. Get feedback. Do a reality check. Is what you think really what's going on?"

COURAGE 4: LET FEELINGS TAKE FLIGHT [4]

"If we don't pay attention to feelings, we can be left with people who feel disconnected from the group, just like what the previous speaker said." John is leaning forward into the camera. "That can lead to all kinds of problems including mental health issues."

As an example, the 1948 U.S. Air Force leadership manual included a look at emotions ("humanness") as one of seven key traits to understanding its people. By 2011, this focus on feelings was gone.

"Think of the role feelings play in the stories we've looked at. Mark and the last Ironman participant late at night. Mark's empathy. That last Ironman athlete was maybe feeling not quite worthy, and a failure. Think of the Norwegian teenage immigrant. That boy maybe felt homesick, inadequate, but hopeful."

COURAGE 5: BE RESILIENT, AND ROCK YOUR WORLD [5]

Key to building courage, he adds, is knowing and dealing with such emotions as fear, shame and inadequacy. Pick yourself up after failure and feelings of failure. That's resilience. "How to do that when you're feeling like crap?" John puts one hand on his hip. "One day at a time. One thought at a time. One small action. Didn't work? Adjust and try again. Repeat. Be gentle with yourself. You're human.

"That's what really separates the men from the boys, women from girls, and everyone else from the others." Forum participants pause from note-taking for half-smiles. But John doesn't appear to see the humor.

COURAGE 6: SHOW IT, TAKE ACTION [6]

"Think of Chief Clarence Louie, and how he's focused on the importance of Indigenous self-responsibility," John says. "Few have talked about it like he has. Also, what does it take to be a Rez Chief for 40 years?"

What it takes, John says, his voice rising, is to be calm even in the middle of tough problem-solving and decision-making. Face tough conversations and behavior head-on. Drill down to solve problems and improve attitudes. Stay curious, involved and committed to improvement. Be open to innovative ideas.

Show courage by doing mental checks: How might I be wrong here? Listen to others ("Tell me more"). Value relationships. That's where the gold is. If you do, your people will feel safe, seen, heard and respected.

"If you don't, both you and those other people are locked up inside yourselves like... like... a treasure chest." He's grasping now. "But the treasure is actually on the outside: your relationships. Do you see?" Forum participants are nodding. "When you're locked up inside yourself, it's easy to blame everyone else."

John takes a drink of water. "Know what you're feeling, and express it. That's tough for a lot of people. Some think feelings are namby-pamby, weak." John's large bulbous nose crinkles as if he's smelling something bad. He sighs and gives a soft exhale.

"It's sticking up for yourself. The honest talk can build trust and respect, and a stronger team. Otherwise, you're suiting up for battle by being critical, cynical, defensive, and creating barriers. That puts people off."

"Think of the Beatles' George Harrison," John says, "going from being affable to really ticked off by thinking he's not being taken seriously as a songwriter. Think of modern-day Prince Harry, Duke of Sussex, taking on his family (the British monarchy) for what he feels is them not sticking up for him and his wife Meghan Markle with the media."

Part of being open is knowing your limits in the group. How do group members see you? What are the group's core values? What does the group see as good behavior? Practice it. Set boundaries. Encourage honesty and good judgment. Being a leader means having faith your group can meet its goals, and having the discipline to get it done. Start small.

"Some people may not be ready to express emotions. They may not even see them," John says. "Take the first story we looked at. The daughter tried to reconcile her mother and grandmother by getting the two of them in the car and driving them to a theater performance an hour away. It just didn't work. They had no prior warning. The mother closed up."

Prepare some key phrases to use such as, "Tell me more about how this is affecting you. I want to understand." Take a break. In your own mind separate the constant critics never satisfied, from the well-wishers who have important but tough feedback.

"There's no pleasing some people," John says. "When they dump on you, and use you as a punching bag, you have three choices: engage, address or ignore. The person may be trying to pull you into constantly meeting their demands. This can get out of control, so be careful. Try to address the issue and involve the person. Otherwise maybe you can ignore it."[7]

John reminds his audience that the whole point of the forum is to keep the door open to the possibility of change. People can change, even the critics. Work to be generally supportive and encouraging. As an exercise, it may be helpful to have group members each jot down their viewpoint, then together share and discuss.

COURAGE 7: FIGHT SHAME WITH EMPATHY – BE TOUGH INSIDE, GENTLE OUTSIDE [8]

Are there some tough emotions surfacing in your group? Face them head on. People tend to want to be accepted so we may pretend, perform, try to please, and/or be a perfectionist (4P's). When that doesn't work and instead we're shamed in public, we may strike out or close down. As a leader, the cure is to show the shamed person empathy: listen, try to understand, and be supportive. This builds trust.

"A really strong and powerful person," John adds, "is tough at core and, at the same time, gentle with people." This person is clear and open. There are no stealth intentions and/or expectations. This person is a curious learner who isn't afraid to make mistakes and learn from them.

COURAGE 8: EGHS, THEM, 7C's, HILS ... HUH? [9]

An acronym is a set of letters useful to remember information. For example, "EGHS" can stand for embarrassment, guilt, humiliation, shame. These are feelings along a spectrum from low to high long-lasting negative impact. They may all make us feel under attack, but shame is the worst. Where there's shame, what often follows is addiction, violence, aggression, depression, eating disorders, and bullying. "It takes two people to make shame, and also two to heal shame," John points out. Together, getting back to core values can help healing.

Unlike the Himalayan villagers, modern societies (in constant flux) know well the confusion that results when people aren't clear about their role. For example, Kye the teacher didn't realize how sensitive his principal was to being shamed in public, even if Kye only meant to create a "townhall" atmosphere in which issues could be aired.

"THEM" can stand for time, heart, energy, funds. Especially the first three are needed to build understanding and trust. Like a camera lens, if you focus on a person's faults you are shaming them and not giving them space. If you zoom out to see the whole person at once, you are seeing both their strengths and weaknesses, as well as challenges. You're respecting the person's dignity.

"7C's" can mean the qualities that help us face our fears and build emotional muscle: calm, curious, confident, courage, clarity, connection, leading to change. "Think Chief Clarence Louie as a 17-year-old who organized sports teams and tournaments. He gradually became skilled in working with all kinds of people in all kinds of situations, balancing viewpoints, and being open to options. He made a name, and built a reputation."

A person without this emotional muscle may shield themselves, run away, shut down, and/or give up.

"HILS" can stand for four useful questions to guide meetings: What happened? What improvements? What learning? What seeking? "In other words," John says, "What's gone on, what are we seeing that's an improvement, what have we learned, and what were we looking for?

"It's also important to prepare for meetings and hard conversations," John stresses. "Don't just go in 'cold turkey.' What! Are you an amateur?? Make notes and go over them, even role-play with a partner. Thinking you can just wing it doesn't fly."

COURAGE 9: YOU'RE IN MY SPACE! (BE AWARE) [10]

When Colonel John returns after a short break, the forum participants appear eager to continue the talk about emotions, courage and leadership. Most are engrossed in preparing their next set of notes, recording, or gaze to one side considering what he'd shared with them.

"We all face group challenges. People are people. Think 'TOPWWTY.'" The participants look blank. "That's an acronym for 'treat the other person the way you want them to treat you.'" Several viewers chuckle.

"Take geo-politics, for example… please," John begins, to more chuckles. "A country that occupies another country – say Afghanistan, for example – is often faced with a culture they don't know. History is full of stories of occupiers who hadn't a clue about the countries they occupy," John says. "It often doesn't go well. It helps to learn the culture. Remember that whatever annoys you may well annoy the other person, if the situation is reversed."

John Mearsheimer, scholar in international relations, has seen this pattern in the relations between Russia, the U.S. and Ukraine. In the lead-up to the 1962 Cuban Missile Crisis, Americans felt threatened by having Russian military forces so close by in Cuba. They felt it was an affront to the Monroe Doctrine. Personal space had been violated. At the time, U.S. President John F. Kennedy supported back-channel mediation efforts. In the end, Russia withdrew nuclear-armed missiles from Cuba, and the U.S. withdrew their nuclear-armed missiles from Turkey.

According to Mearsheimer, in the years leading up to the February 2022 Russian invasion of Ukraine, Russia was sending a clear message to the U.S. to back off. "You either back off [and leave Ukraine as a buffer state]," Mearsheimer said, "or you continue to play these games where you continue to try to make Ukraine a Western bastion on our doorstep, in which case we'll wreck the country." Mearsheimer sees the larger lesson as being, "if you don't recognize what other people think, [if] you're incapable of putting yourself into their shoes, you're going to get yourself into a heck of a lot of trouble."

In other words, acknowledge the other person's interests. But what of the interests of the buffer state itself? John pauses, his eyes dark and distant before continuing, measuring his words. "Let's be clear here. Once violence is unleashed, it is very difficult to come back from the destruction of war. The damage is not easily reversed. The loss of life is tragic and final." His eyes are glassy, his forehead furrowed. "Talks behind the scenes to reduce tensions have the potential power to change history, long before the first gunfire, rocket launchers and missiles.

"Whether it's countries, neighborhoods, or any two or more people trying to get along," he murmurs, his voice low, "the approach is similar. It all starts with the practices we've been talking about. Step by step. Basically, it's important to stay curious and empathetic, to at least listen. Who am I,

PART TWO - MIND, EMOTION & SPIRIT

and who are these people? What are our triggers, history, challenges? How do we tend to operate as a culture, work together? What do we respect? What are our hopes and dreams?"

Key to any group work is being clear about personal values and group values. Clarity sets participants up for feedback give-and-take, respect for the dignity of all, and trust. "Decision-making may get even more challenging not easier," John stresses, "but you gain confidence in knowing you're doing the right thing."

COURAGE 10: TTT, FFEM, VBB ... SAY WHAT? [11]

"Okay, more acronyms," John says. "Don't rush in to tough conversations when you're triggered and upset. Give yourself time, space, silence to calm down. Don't talk, text or type with the other person (TTT)." Slow down and think carefully. Don't just do the fun, fast and easy thing in the moment. (FFEM).

"For a great productive meeting, think VBB," John says. "Core values and appropriate behavior. Set boundaries. Don't shame or blame people. Listen, question and learn. Share your impressions, and take notes to understand. Take a break, then get back to the meeting.

"It's also really important to admit your own faults and the other person's strengths. Check to see that everyone in the group is doing what they're supposed to do. Value people's time, and assume good intention. You're looking for solutions that will help everyone."

If you're facing a meeting in which others will be giving you tough feedback, prepare yourself physically. Aim for high energy: hydrate, nourish, get enough sleep.

COURAGE 11: PRACTICE "BRAVING" FOR TRUST [12]

"Okay, my last acronym." Some participants roll their eyes. Another drops his head on his forearm. John is unmoved. "Before I give it to you, remember that your group will really respect you for doing the right thing, even when doing the right thing is hard. It means going directly to the people involved in a conflict to find a solution. Work together. Be specific."

Trust makes anything possible. Researcher Brene Brown came up with the acronym BRAVING that lists important trust-building qualities: Boundaries.

Reliability. Accountability. Treat confidences like a "vault" (don't gossip). Integrity. No to judging. Be generous (assume good intention).

"Ask for help when you need it, and leaders will trust you more. Trust yourself, too!"

COURAGE 12: MAKE SPACE TO EXPLORE GRAY AREAS [13]

"Okay, getting back to courage," John is nearing the end of his talk. "Taking planned risks is so important. It really broadens your perspective. Stay curious and flexible. Explore those gray areas in life. That can really reduce frustration, resentment and defensiveness in a group. Maybe the reality behind the situation is something you never would have thought."

WSpace unmutes her audio. "Colonel." "Yes," he says brightly.

"I'm thinking that a big part of getting along with a group, finding joy and meaning," she begins, groping for the right words, "is everyone feeling appreciated for what they bring to the group. Everyone is given enough I'll call it 'white space' to relax and be themselves," WSpace continues. "They don't feel pressure to prove something, the ego stuff."

John interrupts, nodding his head vigorously, and gives two thumbs up. "Yes, WSpace, you nailed it right on the head." He addresses the entire audience. "What's hiding behind your fears? Finding out may take you to another level, and open the door to the best, most powerful experiences yet of your life."

* * *

REVIEW:

1. Colonel John talks about 12 tools to build courage. What do you think is the most important tool? Explain your choice.

2. The former submarine commander David Marquet wanted his crew to be "assertive." What does "assertive" mean? How did he help them to be assertive?

EIGHT ACRONYMS *(based on the research of Brene Brown, Dare to Lead, 2018)*

EGHS	*Embarrassment, guilt, humiliation, shame* (I feel under attack.)
THEM	*Time, heart, energy, money* (I give more of these to understand and move forward together.)
7C's	*Calm, curious, confident, courageous, clarity,* *core connection = change* (I practice these daily for positive change.)
HILS	*What happened? What improvements were there?* *What did we learn? What were we seeking?* (These are on our meeting agendas.)
FFEM	*Fast, fun, easy in the moment* (This can lead me away from my *values*.)
TTT	*Don't talk, text, or type* (Give myself *space to cool down:* time, distance, silence, if I've been emotionally triggered).
VBB	*Values, behavior, boundaries* (*Clarity* of values is reflected in appropriate behavior, and boundaries: what's okay and not okay.)
BRAVING (DL p224)	*Set boundaries, be reliable, accountable, "vault" (privacy), integrity,* *no to judging, be generous* (Building *trust* involves these seven key qualities.)

CHANGE

CORE CONNECTION (TRUST)
- BRAVING (BIG 7)
(boundaries, be reliable, accountable, "vault" (privacy), integrity, no to judging, be generous)

CLARITY
- HILS (happened? improved? learnt? seek?) results, specific, focused

CONFIDENCE
- do right thing, not FFEM (fast, fun, easy in moment)
- life experience makes perspective

COURAGE
- a habit
- know self (emotion triggers)
- be open (vulnerable)

CALM
- space (time, distance, silence)
- respectful
- despite EGHS (embarrassment, guilt, humiliation, shame)

CURIOUS
- gray areas
- THEM (time, heart, energy, money)

Seven C's Chart (based on research by Brene Brown, source "Dare to Lead", 2018)

CHAPTER THREE -
Spirit

"Crap happens. Deal with it." T's jaw clenches. "Whose life is it, anyway? It's Tyrone's. How does he want to live it? And what's he going to do about it? Those are the questions."

CONFIDENCE IN INNER SPIRIT

PREVIEW:

1. What is "confidence"? Explain.

2. What do you want in life? What do you think you're capable of? Is there a gap between what you want and your "limiting beliefs"? What's the next step?

* * *

The whole concept of confidence that leads to courage deserved a speaker-talk of its own. BSwan takes to the microphone. BSwan is looking a little rough around the edges, as if BSwan hadn't shaved for the duration of the forum and the lead-up to it, and hadn't slept much as well. Dark circles surrounding black eyes makes them look even more deeply set. Hair hangs limply over forehead, and is pushed to one side, mouth slack.

A rumble from the drone jostles BSwan's coffee cup, and the spoon inside tinkles ever so slightly. "Thank you, Colonel John, for that very thought-provoking talk about emotions, courage and leadership. Please thank your team for putting it together on such short notice."

BSwan gives the participants a 15-minute break, then introduces the forum's next talk. "How can a person prepare for the path of life, instead of wasting time trying to prepare a perfect life path?" BSwan begins, reading from a script and glancing up.

"A smooth life path with no ups and downs, where we don't get hurt, and we don't hurt others. It doesn't exist. The best we can do is teach courage, praise effort, and model grit.[1] Cultures around the world - different in so many ways - generally teach these things."

"Welcome to 'T,' our next speaker." Unlike the rest of the forum guests, T speaks from outdoors somewhere in an urban street neighborhood and from his phone or, at least, someone's phone. The short, slight-built, hunched and wizened old man has grizzled olive-colored skin, black scraggly hair and thick eyebrows. He wears a dark cap and shirt jacket over a crumpled open-neck white button-down shirt. What appears to be a small black flattened stone heart hangs around his neck on a thin black cord.

T has a peculiarly distant look to his dark eyes. After a few minutes it becomes clear he is in fact blind. "I'm going to talk about the Tyrone story, how he tried to re-connect with family," T begins, the sounds of a busy street behind him. "He had some wonderful reunions, but some people weren't particularly interested, even rude, and he felt hurt."

Despite his appearance, T's voice - higher than Colonel John's - is strong and clear. His accent is hard to identify. T could be from anywhere. "Tyrone was dragging himself around afterwards," T continues. "He questioned his worth, purpose and meaning. That's many of us much of the time, and we can spend years even much of our lives like that," T says. "There's an answer, and I'm gonna call it your inner 'spirit.'"

T has no notes, but he seldom falters or pauses. There is no glass of water by his side, only someone apparently off-camera holding the phone so that daylight evenly lights T's face. "Crap happens. Deal with it." T's jaw clenches. "Whose life is it, anyway? It's Tyrone's. How does he want to live it? And what's he going to do about it? Those are the questions."

Each of us have a human spirit within, he continues, that is vastly more powerful than we give it credit, regardless of life circumstances. If given half a chance to shine, that spirit in each of us can accomplish amazing feats,

PART TWO - MIND, EMOTION & SPIRIT

beyond anything we might envision. "So how do we free that spirit?" T goes on. "I'm gonna tell you."

The forum participants are sitting woodenly, not quite sure about this speaker. But at this, they appear to collectively decide about him, and reach for "record" buttons or pens and paper. Tyrone needs to first decide what it is deep in his core he wants out of life, T says, for Tyrone to take advantage of the full 'Spirit Solution.' Do some elimination of the other life stuff. Make some choices. Like the Ice Age theory, what's the most useful to him, now? De-clutter. What does he think he's capable of? Is that belief holding him back? What's his vision ahead? "If he doesn't have a focused vision, the actions of other people can easily throw him off-course."

To decide what Tyrone wants in life, it's important that he take stock of seven aspects: physical body, emotions, relationships, time management, work life mission, money, acknowledging his successes as well as how he helps others. With a focus, he starts building momentum, like a car starting and shifting through gears. Every step builds on the last, to get him to his destination. Regardless of a person's circumstances, a person has control over their state of mind. Every day by their actions, a person chooses suffering or happiness.[2]

"Ya, that sounds really kumbaya," T adds. "But think of a hockey team during a big game. Say, they're behind ten goals. They can get back on the ice frustrated, probably get in a fight, with penalties that leave them in even worse shape: down one or more players."

"Or, they can as a team focus on skill, strategy, and out-play the other side, regardless of the outcome. They decide to channel their energy differently. It's all about state of mind, and what you tell yourself to do. You're in control."

"A sports team uses their bodies to reach their goal," T points out. "But even with the rest of us in everyday life, it's how we use our body - say putting a smile on our face when we're sad - that can help shift our state of mind, by influencing our emotions. Gotta stand tall."

We talk about "needs," T continues, but exactly what are needs? More or less, they're the following. A person: [3]

1. Doesn't like surprises in life, and avoids them OR

2. Craves surprises, and goes looking for them.

3. Wants to be "stand out" important, OR

4. Wants to belong, to be a part of something or with someone.

5. Is growing somehow, AND

6. Is helping others.

"What will help Tyrone," T adds, "is to work with other people to meet his goal, whatever it is. Just like a hockey player on a team, each person benefits from the others."

The focused vision of every sports coach around the world is the same: to win. Every sports coach will have a game plan, whether it's effective or not. The coach may know how to win but, if the team is confused on the best way to prepare, there may be trouble. (For example, different team-members may have different values and beliefs). The coach's job is to get the whole team committed to doing the same preparation in the same way (the same strategy). To do so, the players must be inspired and feel motivated. What'll trigger each player to support the coach? The coach may need to find out if each player has some kind of belief that holds the player back. For example: "I'm working really hard and playing the best I can right now. I can't do any better." [4]

"Tyrone is like that coach, and those team players all in one," T rasps, momentarily losing his voice. "In his life, he's got to make a plan and lead the way like the coach, as well as do the actual game work like the team players." T is coming to the end of his talk. "Tyrone may feel he's holding the remnants of his entire family in his hands, and he's hanging on tight," T has tears in his dim eyes. "Maybe it's time to let them go."

The person holding the phone murmurs to T, "the food bank just opened."

"Okay, thank you. Let's go." The two get up, preparing to leave, and the screen goes black.

Back at the drone, the forum participants are all staring dazed, mouth open. While WSpace, GArea and BSwan think about what they've just heard and seen, BSwan is first to find words. "Thank you, T, and your friend. Have a really good day."

* * *

REVIEW:

1. What are seven parts of life that affect a person?
2. What does "state of mind" mean? What controls it?
3. How is Tyrone like a sports coach and team player at the same time?
4. What core values does T talk about? Explain your choices.

"We are all visitors to this time, this place. We are just passing through. Our purpose here is to observe, to learn, to grow, to love... and then we return home."
-Australian Aboriginal Proverb [1]

BIGGER THAN ME

PREVIEW:

1. How do you explain life? Why and how is it that we are here?
2. What two feelings do you think are the most powerful? Explain.

* * *

Aisha had just gotten off work and is sitting at a warm-coloured wood table in front of a small cheery sun-lit kitchen, still in the work tunic and sweater she wears as a cash-register clerk at the local big-box grocery store.

Aisha is an attractive middle-aged woman, lean and muscular, her tinted dark blonde hair in a very short cut that brings out her large dark merry eyes. She wears no makeup. Her natural eyelashes are long and black, as are the thick eyebrows that dance expressively when she speaks. Aisha's shoulders are broad, but she isn't a particularly tall woman. On this day, her tanned olive complexion is lined and haggard, cheeks sagging. But, when introduced to the forum participants, she brightens.

"Spirit," she begins, her high voice that of a girl. "What does it mean?" Aisha's accent is Middle Eastern.

"We've been talking about that spark inside a person that makes a person a person." Aisha removes her sweater, and settles in. "Look at any plant out in the natural world - a weed, tree, flower - and it's easy to see they each have their own distinctive spark, too. As a seedling, a weed grows in a certain pattern. A particular flower has its own way. So does any tree. Millions of the same species will look the same; that's how it's programmed to grow. How remarkable! Yes, of course we're talking about science. Science describes what we see in front of us."

"And why does it all happen that way? Getting along with others is a bit of a mystery, too." As previous speakers had said, to get along a person must keep an open mind. Don't judge. Be curious to learn. But Aisha adds that doing so opens the door for Life Spirit to work its magic. Some but not all may speak of this life force in religious terms (such as miracles). In any case, "spirit magic" is, at core, out of human control.

In life, Aisha continues, two feelings reign: love and fear. An open mind is loving. A closed mind is fearful.[2] To be open, a person must forgive. To forgive is finally deciding that what happened in the past is done and over. It wasn't okay, and will never be okay. But that was then. This is now. "Also if we're not forgiving we're often judging, and people don't respond well to being judged." Aisha breaks into a hearty laugh. [3]

To forgive, a person must take the time they need to grieve the past, emotionally bring themselves to the present time, and focus on the future. Forgiveness is seeing the other person as bigger than any bad behavior. That other person has the ability to change. And this forgiveness can't be forced. Compassion can't be forced.

"But keep in mind," Aisha continues her eyes serious, "you may show this forgiveness, this love towards someone. But it doesn't mean the other person necessarily belongs in your life. You can hold those two things at the same time - love and healthy separation." [4]

"Getting back to the science thing, here we all are on this planet," she says. "As members of the human race, no one of us has any advantage over the other. No one's 'The Boss.' We're just these human beings who happen to be born. We had nothing to do with it. So we have no real 'authority' over anyone, even ourselves. We can be inspired by the ideas of other people - our equals - and the Spirit of Life in all its mystery. Is there something you need to change about yourself, surrender, transform to be a better person in this world?" Aisha asks, "Are some people threatened by you just being yourself? Do they find you as a person offensive? If that's the case, the best we can ask Life for is protection and humility, and for the strength to keep on being who we are." [5]

Maintaining a calm and peaceful state of mind sets a powerfully positive tone. If you're calm, it'll show in your interactions with others. "Even at the best of times people's emotions are sensitive, fragile. We forget that,"

Aisha reminds her audience. People will disagree with each other. The trick is to be cautious and careful in what we say and do as we move forward through the disagreement. It doesn't have to turn into an argument. Seek to understand them and preserve their dignity. Get creative and collaborate. "When you're really struggling to forgive someone, ask the Life Spirit to take over," Aisha says softly. "Ask the Life Spirit to reveal the hidden love bond, and to make the change that you're having a hard time to make." [6]

Aisha moves to two stories, the first about the power of the dream state (night or day) when the Life Spirit speaks to a person.

According to Indigenous Peoples in Australia, a person who loses the ability to dream is a person "losing part of its soul." [7] Indigenous Peoples in North America, and Africa also value such dreams and their meaning.

A workplace group in Canada was attending a seminar, and explored together their individual dreams from sleep the night before. Each day at the sacred gathering place in the middle of the room, they began with silent "pinakarri" (the Australian Aboriginal word for deep listening through silence and deep breathing). [8]

The group felt connected in a very deep sense as they learned age-old ways of working together, something very powerful and beyond themselves. As the days went on, it seemed that a young Indigenous man was getting more and more excited about the whole process. He was seeing connections between the teachings of his First Nations Elders and the teachings of Australian Aboriginal Peoples from the other side of the world. He was excited to share what he was learning, and wanted to bring these diverse peoples together. After one circle-sharing, the young man lifted his arms from the elbows with hands raised skyward in a gesture of acknowledgment and respect, his eyes bright and shining. [9]

Aisha pauses for a silent moment, then continues with the second story.

A completely different U.S. workshop began with a woman clearly frustrated. She liked the idea of conflict transformation, she said, but hadn't seen it actually work. Around her, men and women of her Quaker faith community looked on from church pews. Another woman was equally blunt, calling previous efforts at conflict transformation heart-breaking and spiritually exhausting. A man said conflict made him feel ill and fearful, and he wanted to get beyond this block. With help from Quakers outside the immediate local group, they gained more understanding and moved closer to a transformation.[10]

Aisha's examples of dreams and a frustrated call for help took Aisha to the next part of her talk. Even the most skilled of us, she says, may struggle with group tensions and conflicts. We all can benefit from help outside ourselves, may benefit from being held in the "Light."

Western liberal Quakers (the Religious Society of Friends) certainly think so. They may believe that God is in everyone, and a core Quaker value is peacebuilding. However, group peace is often a challenge.

"The Quakers say the key to the solution," Aisha says, "is getting back to Quaker roots: the communication process for which they're known." They talk of being open to the spiritual Light that shows and reveals peace. Silence, listening, waiting on inspiration. "Christian Quakers may refer to this Light as God, Holy Spirit, the Christ. Other Quakers may not. The challenge for Quakers remains the same as for anyone," Aisha stresses. "No one wants to be seen as too assertive and 'un-Quakerly,' and no one wants to admit to a conflict that Quakers can't handle. Tough talk and being honest with feelings and emotions, perceptions and assumptions is really hard to do!" Aisha throws her hands in the air in mock frustration. Truth is complex. Pitfalls include avoidance, denial, and ongoing tensions. For Quakers, the aim is less compromise or consensus than "unity in the Spirit" as felt in the "sense" of a gathering. To that end, the goal is to see and hear each person, to ask questions and clarify values, to come to a positive decision for change without imposing hasty policies.[11]

"For Quakers, creativity is crucial," Aisha explains. "Name the problem tactfully, and your perspective. Listen for others' feelings and needs. The intent is also that I be changed myself, that I be open to alternative solutions and the Light."

Aisha's phone rings. A colleague is sick, and Aisha is being called back in to her workplace to cover the shift. Her face falls. She sighs, puts her sweater back on and collects her phone, purse and car keys.

"One question," a forum participant presses a raised hand emoji, and is unmuted. Aisha is getting up, but pauses expectantly. "What if," the man says hesitantly, almost apologetically, "a person doesn't believe there *is* a Life Spirit?"

"Then they don't," she says quietly. "Namaste. The Light within me honors the Light within you." [12] Aisha's smile returns briefly, kindly, before the screen goes dark.

* * *

REVIEW:

1. What does Aisha suggest we ask for, if others are offended by us just being ourselves?

2. How does Life Spirit speak to us, according to Indigenous cultures? When?

3. When working to transform conflict, what third party do Quakers invite to the gathering?

4. What core values does Aisha talk about? Explain your choices.

PART THREE –
Speaking in Black Swan

"It's the old 'can't see the forest for the trees' problem: Where's the forest? All these trees are in my way. Oh! The trees are the forest."

BLACK SWAN SOARS

PREVIEW:

1. What does "random" mean? Is the universe random?
2. If we do everything right, can we guarantee getting along? Why or why not?

* * *

BSwan sits deep in thought. Mind, emotions, spirit. People are so complex. Getting along can be fairly simple if the basic pieces are in place, or not simple if pieces are missing. But even if a person does everything "right," can the person guarantee getting along? Can we really predict anything? In many ways life is quite random and out of our control, like shaking and tossing dice. Which set of dots will we see? Which life events?

"Are you okay?" GArea interrupts. "You don't look very well."

"I'm fine [cough]."

The forum is wrapping up, and BSwan is scheduled as the last speaker. WSpace and GArea look sideways at each other. The two of them have no idea what BSwan's talk will be about, and BSwan doesn't look well at all. Haggard. Eyes dark. Skin gray. Hunched over and hacking. BSwan has physically dwindled over the past few days of the forum, and the two of them don't know why or how. The on-screen participants wait expectantly. BSwan begins.

"Ya over the past week during this forum, we've sort of heard a lot – from different places and cultures - about kind of what it means to get along with others.

"Like how do we get ourselves into conflict, and how do we get ourselves out of conflict? We've come up with some ideas. Now we may go away thinking we've got it all sorted out."

BSwan coughs, takes a slow drink of water, a long sigh, and relaxes shoulders. "That's dangerous," BSwan looks into the camera. "We don't have it all sorted out. What we need to do now is recognize how little we know, and how much of life and the world around us is just plain unpredictable." Forum participants have stopped writing, and are looking up. [1]

"We see men and women and think we know, based on our culture, what it means to be a man or a woman. We don't see what First Nations call the 'two-spirited.' We see gender in rigid terms." BSwan sets the drinking glass down on the table but the glass moves very slightly. No one seems to notice.

"Like what I'm getting at is that much of our sort of decision-making with other people is without really understanding the world around us. People think they know more than they do. And they don't want to admit it when they don't know. We kind of build theory based on experience and science. But like it only takes one exception to shred it to pieces." [2] BSwan's listeners start writing and typing again, others recording.

We have expectations, BSwan continues. But then something will happen in a big way that doesn't meet expectations. We try to explain it afterwards but we really can't. Life's gotten complicated, with technological changes, inventions, unplanned chance connections. It all makes for random complicated causes and effects. [3]

People tend to get stuck in the bits and pieces of everyday life, BSwan adds, instead of zooming out like a camera lens to see the next big impact event that's coming in their lives, and in society. "It's the old 'can't see the forest for the trees' problem: Where's the forest? All these trees are in my way. Oh! The trees are the forest. People are very proud of what they know, how far they sort of feel they've progressed," BSwan says, then stops with a deep hoarse cough. [4]

"But the challenge now is to step down from that arrogance, in all parts of life and society. Where are the knowledge gaps? That's what we need to focus on, and all of us together really taking a gamble, a risk on the unknown. We are so unprepared to handle say pandemics, terrorist attacks, wars. We can't predict the future. We have a really hard time to see cause and effect." [5]

"But," A young man presses a hand-up emoji, and WSpace unmutes him. BSwan cuts in, "I'd like to finish," and the man is silent. The drinking glass is now clearly moving, and BSwan reaches over to catch it from skittering a few inches. It seems the drone is starting up. The floor rumbles and vibrates beneath them.

What human beings need now, BSwan continues, is to become more generalist not less, and focus on developing imagination. Our intuition is overwhelmed by modern life.[6] When we're facing tensions, we need to more consciously explore all parts of the situation and be more open to the unexpected. Close the gap between what we know and don't know. For real.

"Ya, like we need to study the sort of messy reality of the unusual." BSwan is waving hands in excitement. "We need to study the oddball 'severe circumstances' to figure out what to do next, instead of focusing on the usual day-to-day stuff." BSwan now looks deathly gray, mouth gaping open. "It's not always all about what's rational, and what makes sense," BSwan gasps. "At the same time," BSwan adds with another deep wracking cough, "there's great work being done everywhere to make life better, and we need to acknowledge these everyday heroes not getting recognition. It's important for morale." [7]

GArea leans over, grips BSwan's arm, and whispers something in BSwan's ear. The floor is now moving under them, the rumbling louder, but strangely the drone motor is silent.

"Reality is random, unknown, im..improbable, extreme," BSwan blurts out. "Get used to it." With a lurch, BSwan stands and lunges for the bathroom door, heaving. GArea goes after but the door is already closed. WSpace has just enough time to put her iPad into its case, and end the forum on her phone, before the entire drone shifts on its axis.

"Thank you everyone!" she yells, and teeters off her chair to the floor. Then along with everything on the table, a kitchen microwave, small oven and chairs she's tossed to a far corner of the room with GArea. The rumbling is deafening, the shaking earth-shattering.

The bathroom door opens and a massive muscular creature with the features of an arching black swan emerges, its seven-foot wingspan outstretched, eyes wide in fear, neck craning forward, beak open. The jolting continues, activating the door mechanism of the drone. In the time it takes the creature to pry itself from the bathroom cubicle, the drone flips, the door wide open overhead. In the distance trees topple to the ground ripped from their roots.

The swan gawks at the opening above it. It's perched on one corner of the table rolled up against the pile over GArea and WSpace. The bird's webbed feet and long, narrow toes fumble with the strap of WSpace's iPad case. Grabbing it with its broad, flat bill, the swan takes off out through the door. WSpace grabs for traction. Too late. A huge crack has opened in the earth, and the drone tips over the edge into the abyss, debris pouring out the door in its wake.

The swan lifts higher in the forest dusk, disappearing in the distance over the horizon and a darkening lake. A tiny dot falls, the swan apparently unaware, and the iPad is gone with a splash. Then silence.

From WSpace's phone, landing hard against a tree, a tinkling audio notification: "Mom, I recorded the forum for you like you said. What do you want me to do with it?

"Mom?..

"Mom???"

* * *

REVIEW:

1. What does BSwan say humanity needs to do right now? What does this advice have to do with knowledge gaps, developing imagination, and seeing cause and effect?

2. According to BSwan, what does reality have to do with what's rational and what makes sense?

3. What are the core values in BSwan's talk? Explain.

4. What happens to the drone, WSpace, GArea and BSwan?

"Your mom was really passionate about her work," Keen says quietly, not leaving Clarity's eyes. "This could be a way to honour it... and maybe help you to feel better."

AFTERWORD

PREVIEW:

1. Which story in this book did you find most interesting? In what way?

2. If you had to do a group presentation about this book, what would you do?

* * *

Clarity stares out the window, her mouth slack, shoulders stooped. After the tragic earthquake and destruction of the drone, she hadn't gone back to school. Instead, she's mired in shock, numb with grief. Unable to process what had happened. Unable to even cry.

Friends of the family and family members stepped in to be with her for as long as she needed. She's staying in town with some of them, barely leaving her room, binging on streamed shows.

Clarity also watches the forum recording over and over for any glimpse of her mother the co-host, pausing and rewinding the lead-up stories and drone discussions between WSpace, GArea, and BSwan. It's assumed WSpace and GArea are dead, but no bodies have been found. From headquarters there's still no trace of BSwan, who has simply disappeared.

While WSpace was slight-built, Clarity is also white, short, but robust, muscular, with a round freckled face, bright green eyes, and thick short hair dyed orange and green.

Clarity's friend Savvy (a tall, thin Black girl with pasted-on one-inch eyelashes and shoulder-length straight dyed red hair) comes over and fills Clarity in on the day's events. It's their senior year at high school, and should have been exciting, invigorating, full of hope for the future. Instead, Clarity sees no purpose, and shuffles through the weeks.

Keen rounds out their threesome. Clarity and Savvy have known him since kindergarten, a muscular tall white guy with short, wavy blonde hair, a perpetual smile and perfect teeth. His eyes brim with confidence and something else, concern.

"So, Clarity," he catches Savvy's eye. "Ghazali wants like a group project." Ms. Ghazali is the English teacher, an older woman with a raucous laugh, brimming with energy. "It's pretty open but she's after a process of some kind." Clarity looks blank.

"Ya, I know, um.. She's marking for the communication thing. You know, how well we work together to make say an essay and present it orally... or it could be a video, podcast, something we build, that kinda thing."

Savvy sighs. "I haven't a clue what to do, but Keen has an idea... about your mom's forum work." She glances tentatively at Clarity, who stops the spoon in her mug of hot chocolate, mid-swirl.

Keen brings out the written assignment instructions. Over the course of the next hour, he explains his idea. They could make the forum results the focus, and show the rest of the class the highlights in a way their classmates might understand.

"Your mom was really passionate about her work," Keen says quietly, not leaving Clarity's eyes. "This could be a way to honour it… and maybe help you to feel better."

"Okay," she murmurs. "What?" Keen hadn't caught it. A whisper: "Okay."

It's to be an end-of-term project, completed in sections. First is to settle on a plan and write it up, clearly showing who will do what. Last is the formal presentation or product of some kind. In between, they'll each keep a journal of their progress working with each other.

Stage One - The Plan

Over the next week, the three friends meet in Clarity's bedroom after school and hash over ideas about how people get into conflict and how they get out. They feel that's really what it's all about.

The three (Keen and Savvy do most of the talking) decide they'll do an in-class presentation, with Clarity contributing either a video and/or audio piece. Keen and Savvy will work up a disagreement (okay it'll be a verbal fight, really raw) then pick it apart. Clarity will be the moderator.

Afterwards, Keen and Savvy will replay the scene. They laugh as dialogue flows. At one point, Clarity even chuckles.

Stage Two - Vocabulary

Week Two. Keen sighs. The drone material in front of them is massive. He feels completely overwhelmed. "Where do we start?" he says to Savvy one day as they pass in the hallway. "We could do what Ghazali does with our novels you know, um... Okay start with each story and make a little list of the key words, terms, vocabulary – say 10 to 20 words. Like we do with chapters." So they do that.

"Now what?" Savvy says, sitting on the floor and leaning against Clarity's bed. Clarity is propped with pillows against the headboard, texting someone. Keen is also on the floor, his laptop open on his lap. "Okay, let's do the same with the forum speakers." Keen gazes thoughtfully out the window. "They have awesome things to say." He resumes typing with energy.

Stage Three – Comprehension

Week Three. Once they have the key words, Keen and Savvy make their own questions to tie the words and concepts together:

- *"How did Daughter fail in 'Driving to the Queen E'?"*
- *"How is Indigenous worldview different from 1) the West? 2) the Mosuo people of China? 3) the Maragoli (Mulembe) people of Kenya? How are they the same?"*
- *"Back in the British Isles during the 1600s, the English fought with the Scots. How come they didn't fight so much with each other once they both came to North America?"*

The questions pour out of them. At one point, even Clarity pipes up from her perch in bed. "Is it ever right to record someone without their knowledge?" Then later, "To forgive sounds kinda lame. How do you really do it the right way?"

Stage Four – Essay Topic Sentence

Week Four. "Ahh, I'm overwhelmed again." Keen has set the laptop aside, and is flat on his back on the floor, his hair tousled, clutching one of Clarity's teddy bears. "We've gotta write at least one group essay for this thing ya? What are we going to write about?"

"Maybe we should pick one of the comprehension points and write about that." Savvy is painting her toenails white and gray. "What, Clarity?" she adds absently.

Clarity is curled up under her bedcovers watching a music video. "I said, I think we should do that thing: as human beings we've evolved to get things done by sort of disagreeing with each other."

"Huh?" Keen rolls over, and pulls one of Clarity's blankets off her bed and over him.

"Ya," she adds without paying attention. "That Flowered Dress woman said that."

Stage Five – Presentation Plan

Week Five. Their essay's topic sentence is "It's necessary to talk over differences of opinion, in order to bring together viewpoints." It's about then that Savvy and Keen get into an argument and aren't talking to each other. Clarity sighs, writes the first essay draft herself, and emails it to Savvy and Keen. "Okay, but you missed this point," Savvy messages back while Keen texts: "I think you need to say this." They're talking again.

Week Six. As far as the in-class presentation, Clarity will do the "Disagreement is Important" introduction by video conference from her bedroom. She'll stay on screen during Savvy and Keen's in-class dialogue, and ring a bell like in a boxing match, whenever things get too heated and Savvy and Keen need to retreat to opposite ends of the classroom. Time for space. Clarity will use the pause to point out what went wrong, and how they might make it right. The three (even Clarity) are getting quite excited about the Big Day.

Week Seven. Keen arrives triumphantly holding two sets of boxing gloves for him and Savvy that he borrowed from the school phys-ed teacher. The three friends roar with laughter, playfully sparring as they take turns putting on the gloves.

Stage Six – Class Involvement

Week Eight. "Oh ya, Ghazali wants us to involve the class somehow." Keen is abashedly holding his head, peering at Savvy and Clarity between his fingers. "What?" Savvy is hurriedly scribbling answers to a math exercise.

"I know." Clarity pops off her bed onto the floor. "I was reading this awesome book about getting people to open up and give different opinions." During their presentation, Clarity says excitedly, they can pause a few times to have the class vote on how well the argument (discussion rather) is going. [1]

"Hum... interesting." Savvy looks up from the math mess on her lap. "How would we do that?" They could stop at key points, Clarity says. Put a statement on the screen. The students choose from 0 to 5 whether they agree or not. "Everyone in the class can raise one hand at the same time to kind of give their opinion. They show fist for 0, or one to five fingers. Then we can get people to say why they sort of think that way."

"Oo..." Keen on the floor is all smiles, hugging his knees. "I like that."

Stage Seven – Presentation

Week Nine. The day of the presentation, Savvy and Keen are a hit, the class roaring with laughter at their banter back and forth. The kids grow silent to see Clarity on the screen, absent from school most of the year. In preparation, she's spent a long time with the drone forum material and speaks confidently. They listen intently.

Clarity suggests the students, staff and administration could set up a hallway box for anonymous ideas to better get along: questions, activities, thoughts, suggestions from everyone.

She also suggests setting certain hours during the school day (maybe twice a week) where a private space is set aside for mediation of tensions, disputes and conflict. Express frustrations and harms. Identify emotions. Learn problem-solving skills. Train students as circle facilitator volunteers. (Ms. Ghazali nods enthusiastically and takes notes.) [2]

At the end, the students give the threesome a raucous round of applause and whoops.

After the end-of-day school announcements, Savvy and Keen are out the main door before the bus kids. They head down to the local fast-food place for a smoothie with Clarity, and sit in one of the booths chilling, watching the little kids giggling and calling to each other in the play area. "Were we ever like that?" Keen murmurs.

"Me? Never." Savvy sucks noisily at her straw. Clarity gazes with a small smile at her old friend. "You guys wanna get a pizza and watch a movie?"

"Sounds like a plan." Savvy licks her lips. "Ya seriously," Keen is up for it. "Let's see how we do to decide on which pizza and movie. Good luck with that."

The three leave their seats and head out into the late afternoon, the kids still squealing in the play area.[3]

* * *

REVIEW:

1. Clarity, Savvy and Keen do a group project. What do they do? Explain in detail.

2. How do they involve their class?

3. Define the words clarity, savvy, and keen. Which are nouns and which are adjectives?

ACKNOWLEDGEMENTS

I'm very thankful and in awe of whatever Loving Spirit has filled my head, heart and soul over the past two and a half years as I worked through this book project. Three questions bothered me: "How do we get along? How do we get into conflict, and how do we get out?"

So many people have written about conflict. So many interesting leads just fell into my lap that I could never have predicted. I'm truly humbled. My endnote sources are certainly not the only ones out there. All include very wise insights and suggestions. I take full responsibility for any errors involved in this creation.

It's one thing to spend two years obsessed with a book idea. It's quite another to then pass it to other people for their impressions. Wow! I sure felt vulnerable and scared.

My first readers took the task very seriously. They were also gentle and kind. I'm very thankful to Wayne Demerse, Jack Godwin, Matthew Legge, Jay Lind, Lesley Robertson, Florida Town, Ash Walmsley and Keri Walmsley. Your suggestions were hugely valuable to help polish my manuscript. Fantastic!

Two people came to mind from very different groups who added to the mix with their experiences of getting along and thoughts about conflict: Fred Harbinson of the Penticton Vees junior hockey team, and Larry Pidperyhora Jr. of Penticton Toyota. Thank you for hearing me out, and being so willing to add your insights for my book. You rock.

When it came to self-publication as a first-time book author, this former newspaper reporter was still totally at a loss. I had no idea what I was getting myself into! Authoring a book is truly a marathon if not a triathlon (write, edit, publish). It requires single-minded dedication to taking one careful step at a time. FriesenPress took me by the hand, and lead me through the process in a very efficient and professional way. Thank you to Nife Okeowo and the team for your efforts to make "White Space, Gray Areas & Black Swans" shine.

Finally, this is the point in a book odyssey where it all hits home.

I'm shedding some tears here, as I acknowledge with love Don and Ruth Henningson, my mom and dad. (You'd both be very hesitant and shy to be mentioned so publicly.) You were both about working hard, paying attention to the details, having fun, looking after each other and trying to do the right thing. Thinking of you, my siblings and all those who gathered at one time or another around the old round dining table in our lively kitchen, I'm filled with appreciation and joyful memories. Our home was a loving launchpad sending us into the world to get along.

(I am a white, middle-class, heterosexual, cisgendered and able-bodied North American settler of English, Norwegian, Scottish and Swedish heritage, living with gratitude on the unceded traditional and ancestral territory of the Okanagan Syilx Peoples. My gratitude also extends to the Kwantlen and neighbouring Peoples, on whose lands I spent so much of my early years.)

Index

Symbols

3destiny, Indigenous 46-64

Armstrong, Jeannette
academic, activist, artist 49
curriculum (Indigenous) 48
ecosystems (heal damaged) 48
En'owkin Centre (culture, academics) 49
En'owkin School of International Writing (Indigenous) 49
interpreting for elders 48
motivation (dig deep) 48
Slash (1985 first novel) 49
Theytus Books (publishing, Indigenous) 49
UBCO-study in Indigenous language, knowledge (Dr. Armstrong) 49
Whispering in Shadows (2000 second novel) 49

honours
Armstrong, Dr. Jeannette 50
Louie, Chief Clarence 56
Ice Age Tips 46. *See* theory (Ice Age)

Louie, Clarence
be on time 57
Chief (since 1984, age 24) 53
entrepreneur history (Indigenous) 54
job as role model 54
K'il law na (grizzly bear) 53
leadership key 54
money, own paycheque 53
new information (be open to) 57
Osoyoos Indian Band (OIB) 53
responsibility (personal) 54

rez politics 54
speaks mind (*See* whistle blower) 54
strong leadership (5 parts) 55
wage economy (new) 57
straddling two worlds 50, 97

Wilson-Raybould, Jody
1983 constitutional talks 59
born and bred for leadership 60
clarify protections (Indigenous rights) 60
communication (interpersonal, balance) 60
cooperation (challenge) 61
improve legal treatment of Indigenous 61
Indian Act (replace) 60
legacy (family) 59
Minister of Justice and Attorney General (MOJAG) 60
multicultural diversity (judge appointments) 61
negotiation (customized) 60
pressure, alleged (Liberal government) 61
public office 62
rebuild own communities 60
Seneca 64
SNC-Lavalin 61
Swain, Diana (CBC journalist) 61
taped phone conversation 61
traditions put in place (Indigenous) 60
Trudeau, Justin (Prime Minister) 59
Trudeau, Pierre Elliott (former Prime Minister) 59
United Nations Declaration on the Rights of Indigenous Peoples (UNDRIP) 60
Wilson, Bill (B.C. First Na-

tions Hereditary Chief, Aboriginal spokesperson) 59
4P's (pretend, perform, please, perfect)
emot1-leadership 115

A

Acknowledgements 144-145
acronym - definition
emot1-leadership 115
advantage (none)
spirit2-bigger 128
Afghanistan. *See* geo-politics
Africa (Kenya) 21-25
Chagala Ngesa, Stanley (shaman, Quaker) 23
Khaemba, Simon (pastor) 23
leadership (official)
(post WWII, 1963) 23
Maragoli (peace) 22
missionaries
(Chilson, A.B., Hole, E.T.,
Hotchkiss, W.R.) 21
Quakers
(God in everyone) 21
(noisy or not?) 22
Umwahi (shamanic healing) 22
World War I (1914-19) conscription 23
afterword 138-143
1intro
4characters
Clarity, Keen, Savvy 138
Ghazali, Ms. (English teacher) 139
instructions (assignment) 139
plan (written), journal, then present or product 139
project (group, end-of-term) 139
topic (communication process) 139
1plan 139
2vocab
list (key words) 140
research 140
3comprehension
questions (concepts) 140
4essay (topic sentence) 141

5presentation plan 141
6class involvement 142
7presentation (in-class)
box (hallway), mediation
(training, practice) 142
alliance
mind1-trust 97
anger
mind2-wisdom 104
Angmo. See Himalaya
Armstrong, Jeannette. *See* 3des-
tiny, Indigenous (Armstrong)
arrogance
swan 135

B

bad behavior. *See* forgiveness, reconciliation
balance. *See* worldviews, Indigenous
3destiny (Armstrong) 51
3destiny (Wilson-Raybould) 61
matriarchy (Mosuo) 44
Beatles (The) 7-13
album
push for "Let It Be" 11
artsy 9
band dynamic shifts 10
Best, Pete (first drummer) 8
brotherhood 11, 12
candid & ordinary 9
documentaries. See filmmakers
drift apart 11
fans 10
adoration, dogma 10
Beatlemania 8
firecracker (no more live shows) 10
feud over new manager
(Klein, Allen) 11
Harrison, George 7
black eye 10
frustration 11
technician 8
individual contribution
(Epstein, Brian Manager), (Martin, George EMI), (Preston,

Billy keyboardist) 11
leadership
McCartney fills gap 13
Lennon, John 7
  Jesus comment 10
  shot 10
  "Teddy Boy" style 8
McCartney, Paul 7
mothers die 9
Ono, Yoko
  moves from Dakota 11
peacemaking (support) 12
rooftop concert 11
split up 10
Starr, Ringo 7
  All-Starr Band 12
  born Richard Starkey 8
  support role (egoless) 12
studio 7, 11, 12
takeaway tips 13
winning formula 10
work ethic 8
Begin, Menachem (former Israeli
  prime minister). *See* mind1-trust
beliefs (ie limiting)
  spirit1-confidence 124
belonging. *See* circle of safety
  gender 86
  mind1-trust 96
  sports (team) 83
Black Swan (BSwan), background xiii
blame (responsible). *See* fault
blockage. *See* spirit2-bigger
body language. *See* language (body)
brain (science)
  mind1-trust 100
Buddhism
  goddess (Mosuo) 39
  non-attachment (Himalaya) 28
Bush, George W. (former U.S. president). *See* educators disagree
bus (taking the public)
  (Parks, Rosa activist) 7
bus (taking the public) (McCartney, Paul)

equalizer 8
Liverpool 8
New York 8

C

calm
  emot1-leadership 119
  spirit2-bigger 128
camaraderie
  sports (team) 83
capability
  spirit1-confidence 124
Carter, Jimmy (former U.S. president). *See* mind1-trust
cause/effect
  swan 135
Chagala Ngesa, Stanley (Quaker, shaman)
  See Africa (Kenya) 22
change
  emot1-leadership 115
  mind1-trust 100
  spirit2-bigger 128
characters, support:
  Aisha (see spirit2-bigger)
  Clarity, Keen, Savvy (see afterword)
  Colonel John (see emot1-leadership)
  Critic, Rumi, Silky (see mind2-wisdom)
  Flowered Dress (see mind1-trust)
  Gillies, Kye (see educators disagree)
  Mark (see triathlon)
  Matt, Talia (see sports-team)
  T (see spirit1-confidence)
  Tyrone (see grand tour)
checklists. *See* mind2-wisdom;
  See emot1-leadership
  acronyms 120
  circle process 108
  conflict (confront) 109
  needs (spirit1-confidence) 124
  relationship (in action) 108
  Seven C's Chart 121
  trigger 107
choice
  spirit1-confidence 124

circle of safety. *See* worldviews, Indigenous; *See* 3destiny, Indigenous
    Beatles 9
    grand tour 77
    Highlanders 18
    Himalaya 27
    immigrants 20
    Indigenous 15
    Maragoli (Kenya) 22
    matriarchy (Mosuo) 42
    Mongol 32
    sports (team) 84
circle process
    circle sharing 129
    mind2-wisdom 103
circumstances
    spirit1-confidence 123
    swan 136
Civil Rights Movement (American)
    Blackbird (Beatles song) 7
    Parks, Rosa (activist) 8
    protest (planned non-violent) 7
cliques
    sports (team) 83
collaboration (careful, cautious)
    spirit2-bigger 129
colonization. *See* 3destiny
    belong in place/time? 18
    from Culloden to New World 18
    Indigenous owner inhabitants 18
    Kenya (pre-1963) 22
    Royal Proclamation (1763) 18
    treated as underlings 18
comment (drone team)
    3destiny (Armstrong) 51
    3destiny (Louie) 57
    3destiny (Wilson-Raybould) 62
    Beatles (The) 8
    beginning (Indigenous) 14
    drive (QueenE) 5
    educators disagree 74
    gender 87
    grand tour 79
    Himalaya 28

immigrants - Maragoli (Kenya) 24
matriarchy (Mosuo) 42
Mongol 34
slap 85
sports (team) 83
triathlon 67
commitment
    spirit1-confidence 125
    sports (team) 83
communication (process, Quaker)
    spirit2-bigger 130
compassion
    spirit2-bigger 128
complexity
    swan 134
complication
    swan 135
confidence
    spirit1-confidence 122
conflict
    transformation 129
conflict resolution
    forum (format) 93
connection
    grand tour 77, 78
    swan 135
control (out of human)
    spirit2-bigger 128
    swan 134
COP Glasgow (2021) 63
core value(s)
    3destiny (Armstrong) 52
    3destiny (Louie) 58
    3destiny (Wilson-Raybould) 64
    Beatles 13
    drive(QueenE) 6
    educators disagree 76
    gender 90
    grand tour 81
    Highlanders 19
    Himalaya 28
    immigrant 20
    Indigenous 15
    Maragoli, Quakers 25

matriarchy (Mosuo) 42
mind1-trust 101
mind2-wisdom 105
Mongol 37
spirit1-confidence 125
spirit2-bigger 128
sports (team) 84
swan 137

courage
drive(QueenE) 5
emot1-leadership 111
immigrant 20
mind1-trust 98
Mongol 32
outlander status 17

creativity
spirit2-bigger 129, 130

criticism
educators disagree 75

Cuba (1962, missile crisis). *See* geo-politics

culture
mind1-trust 101

culture collision
culture, written (pro's & con's) 51
customs (clothes, language, interaction) 17
educators disagree 69
effective and efficient 17
fit in 17
matriarchy (Mosuo) 42
Mongols 33
Outlander 17-19
1945 to 1743 Scotland 17
Fraser, Jamie 18
novels, Gabaldon 17
Randall, Claire 17
sports (team) 83

curiosity
mind1-trust 98

D

Desert, Sonoma. *See* 3destiny (Louie)
dignity
emot1-leadership 116

mind2-wisdom 104
spirit2-bigger 129

dreamlife. *See* spirituality, worldviews

drive (QueenE) 3-6
Granddaughter 3
Grandmother 3
Mother 3
Queen Elizabeth Theatre 4

drone
turbulence 30

drone team (background) xiii

E

education
Alaqai Beki (Mongol queen) 35
Himalaya 27
matriarchy (Mosuo) 42
mind2-wisdom 103

educators disagree 69-76
acknowledge points (nod or two) 72
authority (respect) 74
behaviors (coworker, boss) 72
body language 71
broken relationship 69
change agent 70
change (work for) 75
collaboration (role of) 72
complaints 70
connection (build, regain) 74
consultation 70
criticism (handling, don't react) 75
develop skills (delegation) 74
Fauci, Anthony Dr. (criticism,
George Bush comment) 74
frustration (role of) 72
humiliation (feelings of) 70
insecurity 73
interaction (power difference) 73
'I' or 'you' (pronoun focus) 70
mediator (role) 69
physical distance (space) 72
plan to think, other view, issue, solution, value 71
"play the game" 70

150   WHITE SPACE, GRAY AREAS & BLACK SWANS

privacy (role of) 72
process (5 steps) 70
reaction (role of feelings) 75
responsibility (personal) 73
rules (enforcement) 70
solutions (process) 74
support (nature of) 72
system (inadequacy) 75
tact (role of) 72
talking it out 69
trust – support (in public) 70

ego
    See Beatles (The)
      Starr, Ringo
    emot1-leadership 119

emot1-leadership 110-121
    1confidence, decision-making 111
    2intentions, expectations 112
    3feelings rule 112
    4listen to feelings 113
    5resilience step by step 113
    6take action 113
    7tough yet gentle (4P's) 115
    8acronym(4) 115
    9(10)acronym(3) 118
    9(11)acronym-trust(1) 118
    9(12)space to explore gray 119
    9awareness (Mearsheimer) 116
    acronym - definition 115
    acronyms (table) 120
    courage 111
    dignity 116
    ego 119
    empathy 115
    engage, address or ignore 115
    exercise (viewpoints) 115
    fault 116
    fear 119
    geo-politics 117
    gray area (explore) 119
    intention (assume good) 118
    interests 117
    leadership 111
    manual (1948 U.S. Air Force) 113

    Marquet, David L. (former U.S.
      Navy Captain) 111
    risk 111
    Santa Fe, USS 111
    Seven C's Chart 121
    shame 115
    stealth (intentions, expectations) 112
    toolkit (12 Tools to Build Courage) 111
    vulnerable 111

emotions
    emot1-leadership 113
    manual (1948 U.S. Air Force) 113
    mind1-trust 97

empathy
    emot1-leadership 115
    mind2-wisdom 105
    triathlon 67

energy
    spirit1-confidence 124

entrepreneur. *See* 3destiny (Louie)

estrangement
    drive (QueenE) 4

ethnologist
    Iroquois (1742, French Je-
      suit missionary) 51

event (big impact)
    swan 135

exception
    swan 135

expectations
    gender 86
    sports (team) 83
    swan 135

experience (past)
    gender 86
    mind1-trust 99
    swan 135
    triathlon 68

F

failure
    emot1-leadership 113

fame
    Beatles (The) 7

family
- drive(QueenE) 5
- grand tour 77
- Himalaya 26
- matriarchy (Mosuo) 38
- Mongol 33

Fauci, Anthony Dr.. *See* educators disagree

fault (error, defect)
- drive (QueenE) 4
- emot1-leadership 116, 118

FDress. *See* mind1-trust
- emot1-leadership 119

feelings (expression of)
- drive (QueenE) 5
- educators disagree 71
- grand tour 78
- spirit2-bigger 128

filmmakers (documentary)
- Chaud, Marianne. *Himalaya, Land of Women* 28
- Jackson, Peter. *Get Back* 12
- Lindsay-Hogg, Michael. *Let It Be* 11
- Schwartz, Mathieu. *In the Realm of Women, China's Mosuo People* 38

flexibility. *See* mind2-wisdom

forgiveness. *See* culture collision
- role of bad behavior 19
- role of grieving 18
- spirit2-bigger 128
- vs reconciliation 18

forum (format)
- green card (TIP Talk) 94
- group (5) 95
- individual (5min) 93
- mind, emotion, spirit (topics) 95
- paper/recording (group submission) 95
- rate each presenter (1-5) 94
- rooms (break-out) 95
- template (GANTT chart) 94
- Tips In Progress (TIP) 94

fragile. *See* sensitive

frustration
- 3destiny (Wilson-Raybould) 63
- educators disagree 72

spirit1-confidence 124

G

gaps (knowledge, focus)
- swan 135

gathering place (sacred)
- spirit2-bigger 129

gender 86-90
- 2SLGBTQI+ (two spirit, lesbian, gay, bisexual, trans-gender, queer, intersex) 87
- attraction 88
- authentic 88
- BBC Newsnight 2015 (Wark, Kirsty) 86
- belonging 88
- bullying, violence 88
- choice, exploration 87
- cisgender 89
- confusion (gray areas) 86
- core values 90
- crimes 88
- definition 82
- diversity 87
- essentialism (negative) 87
- expectations (cultural) 86
- experience (life) 86
- exploration, questioning 88
- expression 86
- gender (birth) 88
- Greer, Germaine (1970s feminist) 86
- identity 87, 90
- illness (mental) 88
- images (media) 90
- intersectional 89
- intersex 88
- jargon 87
- Jenner, Caitlyn (2015 Woman of Year, Glamour magazine) 87
- language (plain) 87
- laws (homosexuality) 88
- misogyny 87
- non-binary 88
- pedophile 90
- point of view 87

spaces and rights (access to) 89

spectrum 87

stereotype 87

suicide rates (2015) 88

TERF (trans-exclusionary radical feminist) 89

TGIF (transgender-inclusive feminist) 89

transgender (pre- or post-operative) 86

transphobia 87

trigger 87

two spirit (Indigenous) 87

understanding 86

generalist (vs specialist)

swan 136

geo-politics

emot1-leadership 117

get along (process)

3destiny (Armstrong) 49

3destiny (Louie) 54

3destiny (Wilson-Raybould) 61

drive (QueenE)

educators disagree (5 steps) 70

emot1-leadership 110

first settlers, Syilx (Okanagan) 49

gender 86

grand tour 80

Himalaya 27

immigrant 21

Indigenous 4

Maragoli, Quakers 22

matriarchy (Mosuo) 39

mind1-trust 99

mind2-wisdom 103

Mongol 33

Randall, Claire (*Outlander*) 17

spirit1-confidence 123

spirit2-bigger 127

sports (team) 83

swan 134

grand tour 77-81

belonging 78

"bull in a china shop" 80

circle of safety 77

communication 80

connection 77

divisions and boundaries 78

fragility (safe circle) 80

"going home again" 78

history (personal) 77

husks, empty (mistook) 79

illusion (safe circle) 80

needs (unmet) 79

relationship 78

respect, support 80

trauma (lingering effects) 80

vulnerability 80

wounds (emotional) 78

gray area

emot1-leadership 119

gender 86

Gray Area (GArea), background xiii

Greer, Germaine. *See* gender

grief

grand tour 77

Highlanders 18

Himalaya 28

spirit2-bigger 128

group (dynamics)

drive (QueenE) 4

grand tour 78

mind1-trust 99

Toyota (car dealership, Penticton) iv

Vees (hockey team, Penticton) iii

guarantee

swan 134

H

Harbinson, Fred. *See* Vees, Penticton

Highlanders. *See* culture collision (*Outlander*)

clansmen farmers, Gaelic, kilts 18

Colloden (vs England) 18

Hadrian's Wall (Roman defense) 18

oral storytelling culture 18

Himalaya 26-31

education as threat 27

migration (pre-history) 26

non-attachment (Buddhist) 28

Northern India (Zanskar) 26

INDEX   153

Sking (village) 27
women harvest barley 26
Himalaya (family)
Angmo (foreign daughter, sister) 26
Katup (30, husband Norbu kidnaps) 27
Kunzes (gramma) 27
Rickzine (80, great gramma dies) 27
Tematargay (grampa) 27
Himalaya (villagers)
Isephel (girl) 27
Sapel (shepherd girl, 13) 27
Hole (surname)
Hole, Edgar T. (1902 U.S. Midwest) 21
Hole, Hans John (1905 Norway) 21
honesty
spirit2-bigger 130

I

imagination
swan 136
immigrant *See* name reputation
Hole, Hans John (Norway)
bicycle goal 21
Indian Act
3destiny (Wilson-Raybould) 60
Indian Act (1927). *See* Loft, Frederick Lieut.
Indigenous Peoples 15
Australia 22, 129
influence. *See* power
mind2-wisdom 106
inspiration
spirit1-confidence 125
spirit2-bigger 128
intentions (good)
3destiny (Wilson-Raybould) 61
drive(QueenE) 6
educators disagree 72
emot1-leadership 118
grand tour 77
interaction
mind1-trust 98
inter-dependence
grand tour 78
Indigenous 15

matriarchy (Mosuo) 39
Mongol 33
spirit1-confidence 125
interests
emot1-leadership 117
mind1-trust 100
intuition
swan 136
invasion (2022 Russian). *See* geo-politics
irony
Beatles (The) 7

J

Jenner, Caitlyn. *See* gender
jobs. *See* 3destiny (Louie)
judgment
mind2-wisdom 103
spirit2-bigger 128

K

Kennedy, John F. (former U.S. president). *See* geo-politics
Kenya. *See* Africa (Kenya)
Khan, Genghis 33, 56
kumbaya
mind2-wisdom 105
spirit1-confidence 124

L

language (body)
educators disagree 71
language (plain)
gender 87
language (role of)
Himalaya 29
settlers, Syilx (1800's) See 3destiny (Armstrong) 51
leadership
emot1-leadership 111
League of Indians (Canada).
See Loft, Frederick Lieut.
life (source)
control (out of human) 128
mystery (magic, miracle) 127
pattern (programmed) 127

why (the big) 127
Loft, Frederick Lieut. 55
Louie, Chief Clarence
    See 3destiny, Indigenous (Louie) 53

M

Maragoli (Mulembe) People.
  See Africa (Kenya)
Marquet, David L. (former U.S. Navy-
Captain). *See* emot1-leadership
matriarchy (change)
    fears re future - elders (culture keepers,
        property, child/senior care) 41
    technology, transportation 40
matriarchy (family)
    couple (self-centred) 41
    Dasha Zuma (mother) 39
    Dawa (cousin) 41
    Dudji (uncle) 40
    father (role) 40
    gramma (matriarch) 40
    mental health (support) 44
    Nakajiaya (great-uncle) 39
    Naka Matsu (teen) 38
    tight atmosphere (help) 41
matriarchy (matrilineal)
    world examples 41
matriarchy (Mosuo) 38-45
    Buddhism
      Daba priests (shamans) aging 41
    Buddhism (goddess) 39
    core value (life from female source) 42
    economy 44
    ethnic group (40,000) 39
    extended family (agriculture, live-
        stock, care re child/elder) 39
    men construction, fishing, kill live-
        stock, war, funeral 40
    men some political and religious
        power (today) 40
    no word "jealousy" in the *na* language
    39
    pros and cons 45
    provinces (Sichuan and Yunnan) 38

researcher (Blumenfield, Tami) 40
    women inherit property (crops, herds) 40
matriarchy (sexual relations)
    come of age (own bedroom) 39
    discretion, no moral judgment 39
    Latami Dashi (VP, Mosuo Culture
        Center), come of age at 21,
        process to choose lover 40
    separate from family, reproduction 39
    walking marriage, flowering bedroom 39
matriarchy (villagers)
    Duma (friend, new matriarch) 41
    Lamu (daughter of neighbour) 39
    Lijazui village, Lugu Lake 38
Mearsheimer, John (geo-politics) 117
mediation
    mind1-trust 97
metaphor(s) biggest stick, camera lens, cold
   turkey, doesn't want to dance, herding
   cats, level playing field, nail it on the head,
   path of life, play the game, punching bag,
   shake and toss dice, walk in their shoes,
   grand tour (see further notes), mending
   fences, bull in a china shop, empty husks,
   going home again, tough nuts, pussycats,
   mysterious river 4, 5, 29, 37, 70, 77, 78, 79,
   80, 97, 107, 115, 116, 117, 119, 123, 134
metaphor(s), key characters
  (WSpace, GArea, BSwan) xvii
mind
    spirit2-bigger 128
mind1-trust 96-101
    alliance-building (allies) 97
    anger shifted 97
    apple (red) 96
    Begin, Menachem 97
    brain (science)
      pattern, rationalize, justify 100
    Carter Center (Jimmy and Ro-
      salynn Carter) 98
    Carter, Jimmy 97
    change (chaos, crisis) 100
    culture 101
    emotions 97

INDEX

group (dynamics) 99
intention 97
interests, positions (why?) 100
mediation (high stakes) 97
outdated, update 100
peace talks (1978 Camp David) 97
photo for Begin's grandchildren 97
responsibility (personal) 97
Sadat, Anwar 97
safety (talking together) 100
space (mental) 98
suicide 99
technique (Carter) 98
tone 97
transparency 97
trauma 100
mind2-wisdom 102-109
    action (table) 108
    anger (pattern) 104
    circle process (table) 108
    clues (triggers) 104
    conflict, confront (table) 109
    dignity 104
    educators Kye and Gillies (goal,
        values, purpose) 103
    flexibility 106
    Four-Way Test (Rotary) 105
    judgment 103
    kumbaya 105
    perseverance 106
    Rumi 104
    saying (Scottish) 102
    silence (power) 104
    trigger (table) 107
    truth (nature of) 105
    ubuntu 103
    values (group) 105
missile (crisis). *See* geo-politics
momentum
    spirit1-confidence 124
money. *See* 3destiny (Louie)
Mongol 32-37
    emotion (13th century)
        tears (not blood, milk, sa-

liva, urine) 36
Khan, Dayan (descendent) 34
Khan, Genghis
    delegate (sons steppes, daugh-
        ters Silk Route) 34
    family as resource (alliance,
        network, strategy) 36
    Gobi Desert 32
    life's eight directions 34
    name, number 34
    nomad, steppes (northwest) 32
    underdog to start (only
        100,000 soldiers) 36
    unmerciful, visionary, persistent 36
    Yesugei 34
Silk Route
    China (Gansu east to Xian) 32
    (Mediterranean, Indian, Mus-
        lim, Chinese) 32
tribal groups 32
women
    13 camps (wives, daughters, sons) 35
    advice (Genghis Khan) 33
    Alaqai Beki (senior queen,
        multicultural kingdom, Chi-
        nese Inner Mongolia) 33
    alliances (tribes), led battles
        (warrior horsewomen) 33
    Borte (wife) - diplomacy 36
    Checheyigen (daughter) 36
    Chinese walls against Queen
        Manduhai (ruled 1470-1509) 34
    first international empire 33
    impact (unique) 35
    lost power after Genghis 33
    manage biggest empire 33
    social threat? 35
Mongolian. *See Mongol*
Monroe Doctrine. *See* geo-politics
morale
    swan 136
Mosuo
    ethnic group. *See* matriarchy (Mosuo)

motivation
    3destiny (Armstrong) 48
    spirit1-confidence 125
    triathlon 68

N

namaste
    spirit2-bigger 131
name reputation 20
    3destiny (Louie) 53
    Angmo (Himalaya) 28
    earn by actions 20
    getting a bad *rap* 24
    good or bad *rep* 24
    immigrant
      background 20
      choices 20
      hope, faith, ignorance, sup-
        port, energy 20
      insecurity 21
      stereotype 20
    Khan, Genghis (organizer, custom) 34
    pride in heritage 24
    3destiny (Wilson-Raybould) 60
    That which we call a rose, By any other word
      would smell as sweet. (Shakespeare,
      Romeo & Juliet, Act2, Scene2) 24
needs
    drive (QueenE) 5
    grand tour 79
    spirit1-confidence 124
    sports (team) 83

O

Obama, Barack (COP Glasgow 2021) 63
offensive (triggers others)
    spirit2-bigger 128
Old-New World/ Ancestral 17
oral cultures (storytelling)
    3destiny (Armstrong) 48
    Highlanders 18
    Indigenous 15
    Maragoli 22
    Mongol 35

Outlander. See culture collision

P

Parks, Rosa (activist) *see* Civil Rights Movement 7
peace
    education (Kenya) 23
    talks (1978 Camp David) 97
Peoples, Indigenous 15
perseverance
    mind2-wisdom 106
Pidperyhora, Larry Junior.
    See Toyota, Penticton
pinakarri. See worldviews (common links)
    spirit2-bigger 129
pitfalls (avoid, deny)
    spirit2-bigger 130
point of view
    gender 87
positions
    drive (QueenE) 5
    educators disagree 69
    mind1-trust 100
power
    alliances (Mongol) 35
    in numbers (Kenya) 25
    in prosperity (West) 25
    matriarchy-matrilineal (Mosuo) 39
prediction
    swan 134
privilege
    Beatle hops bus 7
progress (proud of)
    swan 135
protection (self)
    spirit2-bigger 128

Q

Quakers (Religious Society of Friends)
    Africa (Kenya) 21
    communication process 130
    population (2017) 22
    sense of gathering (unity in Spirit) 130
    Western liberal 130

Queen Elizabeth Theatre. *See* drive (QueenE)
quick fix 5

R

random
swan 134
rational. *See* sense
reality
swan 136
reconciliation. *See* forgiveness; *See* culture collision
3destiny (Wilson-Raybould) 63
drive(QueenE) 4
reputation. *See* name reputation
reservation (U.S.) 54
reserve (Canada) 54
resilience
emot1-leadership 113
resolution (conflict). *See* conflict resolution
respect and trust
3destiny (Louie) 53
3destiny (Wilson-Raybould) 62
culture collision 17
drive(QueenE) 4
educators disagree 69
grand tour 80
Himalaya 26
Maragoli, Quakers 22
matriarchy (Mosuo) 39
mind1-trust 96
mind2-wisdom 105
responsibility (personal)
3destiny (Louie) 54
educators disagree 73
mind1-trust 97
rez politics. *See* 3destiny (Louie)
rigidity
swan 135
risk
swan 135
triathlon 68
role
emot1-leadership 116
sports (team) 83

Rotary International service
club. *See* mind2-wisdom
Rumi
mind2-wisdom 103
Russia. *See* geo-politics

S

Sadat, Anwar (former Egyptian
president). *See* mind1-trust
safety
mind1-trust 100
Santa Fe, USS (U.S. nuclear submarine). *See* emot1-leadership
science
spirit2-bigger 127
swan 135
sense (make, rational)
swan 136
sense of humour
Beatles (The) 7
sensitive
spirit2-bigger 128
separation (healthy)
spirit2-bigger 128
shame
emot1-leadership 115, 116
significance
triathlon 68
silence
mind2-wisdom 104
Silky. *See* mind2-wisdom
slap 84-86
Academy of Motion Picture
Arts and Sciences 85
alopecia areata (skin disorder) 85
audience (15.36 million) 84
comedy (stand-up) 86
composure, lose 85
defend, in defense of (wife's honor) 85
humiliation (feeling) 85
joke (1997 "G.I. Jane", Demi Moore) 85
Los Angeles (Dolby Theatre) 85
reaction (social media) 85
resigned from Academy (10-

year event ban) 85
Rock, Chris (comedian, 2022 co-
host, Academy Awards) 84
Smith, Jada Pinkett (Will's wife) 85
Smith, Will (2022 Best Actor,
Academy Awards) 84
triggered 85
violence unacceptable 85
SNC-Lavalin. *See* 3destiny
(Wilson-Raybould)
space
mind1-trust 98
speaks mind (whistle blower).
See 3destiny (Louie)
spirit1-confidence 122-126
actions 124
aspects (7) 124
beliefs (limiting) 124
beliefs, values (differences) 125
body (use to influence emotion) 124
capability 124
choice (suffering, happiness) 124
circumstances (life) 123
coach, team players 125
commitment 125
confidence 122
crap happens 123
energy (channel) 124
frustration 124
grit 123
inspired, motivated 125
inter-dependence 125
momentum (build) 124
needs (checklist) 124
spirit (human) 123
state of mind (control over) 124
vision (focused) 124
worth, purpose, meaning 123
spirit2-bigger 127-131
"circle-sharing" 128
"sense" of a gathering (unity
in the Spirit) 129
advantage (none) 128
behavior (bad) 128

blockage 129
bond (hidden love) 129
careful (cautious, creative, collaborate) 129
change (ability to) 128
communication (process, Quaker) 130
compassion (unforced) 128
control (out of human) 128
creativity 130
dream state (power, soul) 129
feelings (open love, closed fear) 128
forgiveness 128
fragility (sensitive) 128
gathering place (sacred) 129
grief 128
guidance (Life Spirit) 129
honesty 130
Indigenous (Australia) 129
inspiration (ideas, insights) 128
judgment 128
Light (hold in the) 130
mind (open, closed) 128
mystery (magic, miracle) 127
namaste 131
offensive (self protection, humility, strength) 128
pattern (programmed) 127
pinakarri (listen, silence, breath) 129
pitfalls (avoid, deny) 130
policies (not hasty) 130
Quakers (Western liberal) 130
science 127
seen and heard (question, clarify) 130
separation (healthy) 128
solutions (alternate) 130
spirit 127
state of mind (calm, peaceful) 128
surrender 128
tact 130
tensions (group) 130
transformation (conflict) 129
values 131
why (the big) 127
spirituality

dream state (power, soul) 129
drive(QueenE) 4
guidance (Life Spirit) 129
Himalaya 28
Indigenous 16
Maragoli, Quakers 23
matriarchy (Mosuo) 39
spirit2-bigger 129
sports (team) 82-84
atmosphere 83
behavior, group 83
belonging 83
camaraderie 83
cliques 83
commitment (nature of) 83
competition 83
examples 82
expectations 83
recreation 83
ringer 83
role (move, react, anticipate) 82
winning (role of) 83
state of mind
spirit1-confidence 124
spirit2-bigger 128
stealth (expectations, intentions). *See* emot1-leadership
suicide
mind1-trust 99
support
grand tour 77
triathlon 66
surrender
spirit2-bigger 128
swan 134-137
arrogance 135
cause/effect 135
circumstances (oddball, severe) 136
complexity 134
complication (society) 135
connections (unplanned, chance) 135
control (out of human) 134
event (big impact) 135
exceptions (experience, science) 135

expectations 135
gamble (risk, unknown) 135
gaps (knowledge, focus) 135
generalist (vs specialist) 136
guarantee (no) 134
heroes (everyday) 136
imagination 136
intuition 136
morale (acknowledge) 136
prediction 134
progress (proud of) 135
random 134
rational (makes sense) 136
reality (messy) 136
rigidity 135
technology (invention) 135

T

tables. *See* checklists
tact
educators disagree 72
spirit2-bigger 130
talking piece (stick)
Maragoli (Kenya) 22
mind2-wisdom 103
worldview (common) 22
taped phone conversation
3destiny (Wilson-Raybould) 61
teacher. *See* educators disagree
technology (invention)
swan 135
tensions (ongoing)
spirit2-bigger 130
theory (Ice Age)
most useful, most sense 46
Toyota, Penticton iv
transformation
spirit2-bigger 128
transparency
mind1-trust 97
trauma
grand tour 80
mind1-trust 100
triathlon 65-68

3.8km swim, 180km bike, 42km
   run (17 hrs) 65
aid station volunteers 65
competition 67
cow bells 66
empathy 67
motivation, past experience 68
risk 68
significance, (role of) 68
support 68
vulnerability 67
trigger
   gender 87
   mind2-wisdom 104
trust. *See* respect and trust 4
truth
   mind2-wisdom 105
Turkey. *See* geo-politics
Turtle Island (Canada) 51.
  See 3destiny, Indigenous

U

ubuntu
   mind2-wisdom 103
Ukraine. *See* geo-politics
Umwahi. *See* Africa (Kenya)
understanding. *See* circle of safety, core values
unionism, early *See* name reputation
   low-wage manual labourers 21
U.S. *See* geo-politics

V

value(s). *See* core value(s)
Vees, Penticton iii
viewpoint. *See* point of view
vision
   spirit1-confidence 124
vulnerability
   grand tour 80
   triathlon 68

W

whistle blower

Bryce, Peter, Dr. (Chief Medi-
   cal Officer, 1907) 54
Loft, Frederick Lieut. (Mohawk,
   Six Nations, WWI) 55
White Space (WSpace), background xiii
Williamson, Marianne "mysterious river" 4
Wilson-Raybould, Jody. *See* 3destiny,
  Indigenous (Wilson-Raybould)
women
   balance (Wilson-Raybould) 61
   Himalaya 27
   Iroquois (*Haudenosaunee*) 51
   matriarchy - matrilineal (Mosuo) 39
   Mongol (raised to rule) 33
   worldviews, Indigenous 15
worldviews (common links)
   circle, talking stick (dreamlife, hopes) 22
   oral traditions (listening, com-
     munity life) 22
   pinakarri (Aborigine) 22
   rites of passage "initiation forest" 22
   soul in nature 22
worldviews, Indigenous 14
   balance (women teach, promote) 15
   four quadrants 15
   circle concept to transform conflict 16
   education when ready 16
   inter-dependence 15
   knowledge
     (self, Elders, Spirits/dreams) 16
   learning, self, balance, beauty 15
   physical, emotional, mental, spiritual 15
   sacred wheel (stone, logos, drums, art) 15
   two spirit (non-binary gender) 15
World War I
   Kenya 23
   Loft, Frederick Lieut. (Canada) 55
World War II
   Kenya 23

ENDNOTES

Hyperlinks were working in 2024 at publication. If links are broken, search Internet Archive (archive.org) or a search engine to find the content.

THOUGHTS FROM THE BENCHES

[1]-"Coaching Staff & Hockey Operations." *Penticton Vees.*
https://www.pentictonvees.ca/coaching-staff
-"Great Moments In Hockey History: 1955 Penticton Vees." Mar 25, 2013.
GreatestHockeyLegends.com
https://www.greatesthockeylegends.com/2013/03/great-moments-in-hockey-history-1955.html
-"BCHL History (2010s)". *bchl.* https://bchl.ca/bchl-history-2010s
-Fred Harbinson email, Nov 10, 2023

[2]-Michaels, Kathy. "Suspected arsonist arrested for Penticton Toyota inferno." *Global News.*
May 9, 2023. https://globalnews.ca/news/9685053/penticton-toyota-inferno-arrest/
-Powrie, Chelsea & Richardson, Casey. "Penticton Toyota team devastated by morning fire, looks ahead to build back better." *Castanet.com.* May 11, 2022. Update 12:05 p.m.
https://www.castanet.net/news/Penticton/368613/Penticton-Toyota-team-devastated-by-morning-fire-looks-ahead-to-build-back-better
-Fast, Taya. "Major fire destroys Toyota dealership in Penticton." *Global News.* May 11, 2022. https://globalnews.ca/video/
rd/1de58e12-d188-11ec-884a-0242ac110005/?jwsource=cl
-Larry Pidperyhora Jr. email Nov 10, 2023.

CHARACTERS

[1]-Soegaard, Mads. "The Power of White Space in Design." *Interaction Design Foundation.*
2021. https://www.interaction-design.org/literature/article/the-power-of-white-space
-Williamson, Marianne. *Everyday Grace: Having Hope, Finding Forgiveness, and Making Miracles.* New York: Riverhead Books. 2002.
-Voss, Chris. "Chris Voss Teaches the Art of Negotiation." *Masterclass.*
https://www.masterclass.com
-Sinek, Simon. *Leaders Eat Last: Why Some Teams Pull Together and Others Don't.* Portfolio. 2014.

-"White Space (Visual Arts)." *Wikipedia, The Free University.* Dec 15, 2023.
    https://en.wikipedia.org/wiki/White_space_%28visual_arts%29

[2]-Sinek, Leaders Eat Last.
    -"gray area." Dictionary. *Merriam-Webster.com* Jan 25, 2024.
    https://merriam-webster.com/dictionary/gray%20area

[3]-Taleb, Nassim Nicholas. *The Black Swan: The Impact of the Highly Improbable. With a new section 'On Robustness and Fragility'* Incerto Series. Second Edition. Random House. 2010.
    -"What are Black Swan Events?" Reshaping Wicked Problems. Unconference. ASU *Shaping EDU. YouTube.* 2021. https://www.youtube.com/watch?v=sZy13hZeq40

PART ONE – FAMOUS OR UNSUNG

CHAPTER ONE – COMING TOGETHER

DRIVING TO THE QUEEN E
[1]Williamson, Everyday Grace. 58.

FOUR GUYS
[1]Jackson, Peter. *Get Back.* Documentary series. Disney Plus. 2021.
    https://www.disneyplus.com/en-ca

[2]Parrott, Les. "Cameraman reveals what the Beatles were like behind the scenes." *60 Minutes Australia. YouTube,* Nov 21, 2021. https://youtu.be/_uYiFiP9snw

[3]-McCartney, Paul. "Paul McCartney: The Waterstones Interview." *Waterstones. YouTube,* December 2, 2021. (Video 55:36-56:44) waterstones.com https://youtu.be/chROemnJflo
    -"Rosa Parks". *Wikipedia.* https://en.wikipedia.org/wiki/Rosa_Parks

[4]Rothman, Lily & Aneja, Arpitha. "You Still Don't Know the Whole Rosa Parks Story." *Time Magazine.* Nov 30, 2015. https://time.com/4125377/rosa-parks-60-years-video/

[5]Jones, Dylan. "At home with Paul McCartney: His most candid interview yet." *GQ Magazine.* Aug 4, 2020. https://www.gq-magazine.co.uk/culture/article/paul-mccartney-interview

[6]-The Cosmiks. "Sean Ono Lennon- John Lennon At 80." *YouTube.* Audio interview Paul McCartney (44:38). Oct 3, 2020. https://youtu.be/uSN40wcgg3k
    - Smithfield, Brad. "Teddy Boys were the Dandies of the 1950s – The British subculture, inspired by the Edwardian Era." *The Vintage News.* Dec 31, 2015. (*See* Further Notes)

[7]-Rubin, Rick. "McCartney 3 2 1." Documentary Series. *Hulu* 2021. https://www.hulu.com
    -"Cameraman reveals." 60 Minutes Australia.

[8]"The Beatles." *Wikipedia.* https://en.wikipedia.org/wiki/The_Beatles

[9]-Gladwell, Malcolm. *Outliers: The story of success.* Boston: Little, Brown and Company. 2008.
    -Trakin, Roy. "Director Michael Lindsay-Hogg on the Long and Winding Road From 'Let It Be' to 'Get Back.'" *Variety* Dec 10, 2021.

https://variety.com/2021/music/news/
michael-lindsay-hogg-director-let-it-be-get-back-1235130999/

[10]Sinek, Leaders Eat Last.

[11]"The Beatles: We Can Work It Out." *The Beatles You Tube Channel*. Vevo. Nov 4, 2015. Song released Dec 1965. https://www.youtube.com/watch?v=Qyclqo_AV2M

[12]-"Julia Lennon Dies." *Beatles Bible*.
https://www.beatlesbible.com/1958/07/15/julia-lennon-dies/
-"Paul McCartney's Mother Mary Dies." *Beatles Bible*.
https://https://www.beatlesbible.com/1956/10/31/paul-mccartneys-mother-mary-dies

[13]-Rubin, McCartney 3 2 1.
- Star, Ringo. "Ringo Starr Says 'Peace and Love' Every Day and Still Believes in the [Message]".
The Late Show With Stephen Colbert. *CBS*. Mar 16, 2021.
https://www.cbs.com/shows/video/FduhX2vxliJlpOEWrHt8Gk9EgaVpf_oB/

[14]"Paul McCartney – Larry King Interview". *YouTube. Larry King Live. CNN*.
(5:13). Part 1 of 8. June 12, 2002. https://www.youtube.com/
watch?v=aW0q5XDjeuA&t=57s
-Rubin, McCartney 3 2 1.

[15]"The Beatles Timeline." *Wikipedia*. https://en.wikipedia.org/wiki/The_Beatles_timeline

[16]Jackson, Get Back.

[17]The Beatles Timeline.

[18]Jacob, Mary K. "Yoko Ono leaves NYC after 50 years, moves to farm purchased with John Lennon." *New York Post*. Feb 24, 2023.
https://nypost.com/2023/02/24/yoko-ono-leaves-nyc-for-a-farm-she-bought-with-john-lennon/

[19]-The Beatles Timeline.
- Trakin, The Long and Winding Road.

[20]-The Beatles Timeline.
-Schaal, Erick. "How Old Were The Beatles When The Band Broke Up?" *ShowBiz Cheat Sheet*. April 19, 2019. https://www.cheatsheet.com/entertainment/how-old-were-the-beatles-when-the-band-broke-up.html/
-Dammann, Luke. "How The Beatles Officially 'Broke Up' At Disney World." *Walt Disney World*. Feb 3, 2022.
https://insidethemagic.net/2022/02/how-beatles-broke-up-disney-ld1/
-Kielty, Martin. "Beatles breakup document expected to sell for $500,000." *Ultimate Classic Rock*. June 25, 2023. https://ultimateclassicrock.com/beatles-breakup-document-auction/
-Laney, Karen 'Gilly.' "John Lennon officially ended the Beatles at Disney World." *Ultimate Classic Rock*. Sept 25, 2011.
https://ultimateclassicrock.com/john-lennon-ended-beatles-at-disney/
-Lindley, Simon. "Contract which officially broke up The Beatles to sell at Sotheby's."

Dec 14, 2018.

https://news.justcollecting.com/

contract-which-officially-broke-up-the-beatles-to-sell-at-sothebys

[21]-Lennon, John. "John Lennon on Dick Cavett (entire show) September 11, 1971." *YouTube*. *The Dick Cavett Show*. 1:45. Sept 11, 1971.

https://www.youtube.com/watch?v=7kXCnKfdGOY

- Larry King Live. McCartney. Part 2, 00:36-1:20 minutes.

[22]McCartney, Paul. "The Woman Who Saved Paul McCartney." *YouTube*. *60 Minutes Australia*. 9:54 minutes. 1991. May 16, 2019. https://youtu.be/dkHEf--YNng

[23]-Harrison, George. "Season 1, Episode 9: Rock Icons – George Harrison." *YouTube*. *The Dick Cavett Show*. Nov 23, 1971. https://www.youtube.com/watch?v=44iIM8GufCI

-Jackson, Get Back.

[24]Colbert, Ringo Starr.

[25]-"Ringo." *Independent*. Oct 28, 1995. https://www.independent.co.uk/life-style/ringo1579907.html

- Colbert, Ringo Starr.

[26]"Peter Jackson Reveals How He Convinced Beatles Paul and Ringo To Let Him Make 'Get Back'." 5:14-5:48 minutes. *YouTube*. *Variety Doc Dreams*. *National Geographic Documentary Films*. 2021. https://www.youtube.com/watch?v=K95MlzDth_A

[27]Wong, Brittany. "What The Beatles Documentary 'Get Back' Can Teach Us About Collaboration: Here's how the Beatles got their creative groove back in Peter Jackson's new documentary." *Huff Post*. Dec 2, 2021.

https://www.huffpost.com/entry/things-the-new-beatles-doc-can-teach-us-about-working-with-otherscollaboration_l_61a66021e4b0451e550d7279

CHAPTER TWO – CULTURE SPEAKS

BACK TO THE BEGINNING

[1]Joseph, Bob. "What is An Indigenous Medicine Wheel?" *Indigenous Corporate Training Inc.* May 24, 2020 https://www.ictinc.ca/blog/what-is-an-indigenous-medicine-wheel

[2]"Aboriginal Worldviews and Education." *Coursera*. Jean-Paul Restoule. University of Toronto. Author earned certificate Fall 2021. https://www.coursera.org/learn/aboriginal-education

[3]Aboriginal Worldviews.

CULTURE WARP

[1]Gabaldon, Diana. "Outlander." 1991. *Starz television series adaptation.* 2014-2023. Season 1. 2014. https://www.starz.com/us/en/series/outlander/21796

[2]Newsroom. "Outlander: What Was Life Really Like for Highland Clansmen?" *The Scotsman.* Update Mar 5, 2016. https://www.scotsman.com/arts-and-culture/film-and-tv/outlander-what-was-life-really-like-for-highland-clansmen-1481531

[3]-"Hadrian's Wall. Construction." *Wikipedia.* 2023.
https://en.wikipedia.org/wiki/Hadrian%27s_Wall#Purpose_of_construction
-"Significance of Hadrian's Wall," *English Heritage.*
https://www.english-heritage.org.uk/visit/places/hadrians-wall/hadrians-wall-history-and-stories/history/significance/

[4]"Jamie Admits to Being a Virgin." Outlander. Season 1, Episode 6.

[5]"America the Beautiful." Outlander. Season 4. Episode 1.

[6]-Joseph, Bob. *21 Things You May Not Know About the Indian Act: Helping Canadians Make Reconciliation with Indigenous Peoples a Reality.* p29. Port Coquitlam: Indigenous Relations Press. 2018.
-Joseph, Things About Indian Act. 84

[7]-Linda & Doug. "Brené Brown on 'Rumbling with Forgiveness.'" *Emotional Affair Journey* Sept 2015. https://www.emotionalaffair.org/brene-brown-on-rumbling-with-forgiveness/
-Westover, Tara. "You Can Love Someone & Still Choose to Say Goodbye" *YouTube.* *SuperSoul Sunday.* OWN. May 5, 2019. https://youtu.be/BS0P1ovIRos
-Legge, Matthew. *Are We Done Fighting?: Building Understanding in a World of Hate and Division.* Gabriola Island: New Society Publishers. 2019.
-personal communication. Oct 12, 2023.

CROSSING OCEANS AND CROSSING PATHS

[1]Oral and archival family history (Henningson, Olund)

[2]-Chagala Ngesa, Stanley. "Quaker Christianity in Kenya." *Friends Journal.* Oct 1, 2019.
https://www.friendsjournal.org/quaker-christianity-in-kenya/
-"Mission in Kenya." *Quakers in the World.* Source: Rasmussen, Ane Marie Bak. "A History of the Quaker Movement in Africa." London: British Academic Press, 1995.
-Wafula, Robert J. "From Mud Huts to Yearly Meetings." *Christian History magazine* 117, The Surprising Quakers, Christian History Institute. 2016.

[3]Chagala Ngesa, Quaker Christianity in Kenya.

[4]-Chagala Ngesa, Quaker Christianity in Kenya.
-"Dragon Dreaming Project Design." Ebook. Version 2.09. 2020. (pinakarri, p9-10) https://dragondreaming.org/wp-content/uploads/2020/01/DragonDreaming_eBook_english_V02.09.pdf

[5]"The Future of Quakerism Belongs to Kenya: How 100,000 Kenyans are redefining what it means to be a Quaker." *Roads & Kingdoms.* April 20, 2016.
https://roadsandkingdoms.com/2016/the-future-of-quakerism-belongs-to-kenya/

[6]"Finding Quakers Around the World." *Friends World Committee For Consultation (FWCC)*. 2017. https://fwcc.world/resources_cpt/map-finding-quakers-around-the-world/

[7]-Mission in Kenya.

-Wafula, From Mud Huts.

-"Quakers in Africa." *Wikipedia*. Last edited Sept 20, 2021. https://en.wikipedia.org/wiki/Quakers_in_Africa

-"What is Friends Church Kenya?" *Friends United Meeting*. Oct 21, 2020. https://www.friendsunitedmeeting.org/news/what-is-friends-church-kenya

-Wafula, From Mud Huts.

[8]Chagala Ngesa, Quaker Christianity in Kenya.

[9]"Friends Schools in Kenya from 1902 to independence in 1963." *Quakers in the World*. https://www.quakersintheworld.org/quakers-in-action/149

[10] Future of Quakerism.

-Chagala Ngesa, Quaker Christianity in Kenya.

[11]Staff blog, Carrie. "A rose by any other name…." Learning English Blog. *BBC*. Mar 4, 2010. [William Shakespeare, "Romeo & Juliet", Act2, Scene2] https://www.bbc.co.uk/blogs/learningenglish/2010/03/a-rose-by-any-other-name.shtml

HIMALAYAN WOMEN MAKING IT WORK

[1]"Global Human Journey." Human Migrations. Education. *National Geographic Magazine*. Jan 2013. https://education.nationalgeographic.org/resource/global-human-journey/

[2]John, Molly. "The World's Tallest Mountain Ranges." *WorldAtlas*. Feb 17, 2021. https://www.worldatlas.com/articles/the-world-s-tallest-mountain-ranges.html

[3]-Chaud, Marianne. *Himalaya, Land of Women. YouTube. SLICE. ZED. ARTE France*. documentary. https://www.youtube.com/watch?v=NPic_MsN-y8

-*Himalaya, Land of Women. YouTube*. SLICE. official trailer. Mar 5, 2020. https://www.youtube.com/watch?v=ywDTRVByw7E

[4]Chaud, Land of Women (doc). 2:54

[5]Chaud, Land of Women (doc). 44:52

[6]Chaud, Land of Women (doc). 41:40

[7]Chaud, Land of Women (doc). 41:40

[8]"Zanskar Valley – Ultimate Travel Guide 2023." *Nomads of India*. https://nomadsofindia.com/travel-guides/zanskar-valley-ultimate-travel-guide/#Frequently_Asked_Questions_FAQs

[9]"Angmo." *Names.org* https://www.names.org/n/angmo/about

MONGOL QUEENS

[1]Weatherford, Jack. *The Secret History of the Mongol Queens: How the Daughters of Genghis Khan Rescued His Empire*. p48. New York: Crown Publishing Group. 2010.

[2]Weatherford, Mongol Queens. back cover, 50-52, 54.

[3]Weatherford, Jack. *The Secret History of the Mongol Queens: How the Daughters of Genghis Khan Rescued His Empire.* Written intro, para2. Random House Audio. Feb 16, 2010.

[4]Weatherford, Mongol Queens. 193, 211, 230, 262, 277.

[5]Weatherford, Mongol Queens. xv, 40, 83-4.

[6]Weatherford, Mongol Queens. xiii, xv, 84.

[7]Weatherford, Mongol Queens. 84-5.

[8]Weatherford, Mongol Queens. xiv-xv, 70-72.

[9]Weatherford, Mongol Queens. xii-xiii, 72-73.

[10]Weatherford, Mongol Queens. 47, 58.

[11]Weatherford, Mongol Queens. 50.

[12]Weatherford, Mongol Queens. 53.

[13]"Mongolian cuisine." *Wikipedia.* https://en.m.wikipedia.org/wiki/Mongolian_cuisine

CHINA'S LAST MATRIARCHY

[1]Schwartz, Mathieu. *In the Realm of Women: China's Mosuo People.* Arte France. *Internet Archives – DocFilm* – In the Realm of Women – China's Mosuo People (Deutsche Welle) (uploaded by TV Archive January 24, 2022). Accessed Jan 28, 2024. https://archive.org/details/ DW_20220124_181500_DocFilm_-_In_the_Realm_of_Women_-Chinas_Mosuo_People

[2]*The Kingdom of Women Part 2* (CCTV 9 Documentary). Special Edition Feb 27, 2016. *China Central Television.* 1:50-1:59, 2:18, 2:25, 2:46
https://www.youtube.com/watch?v=iep_2ZsMHAo
-Kingdom of Women2. 6:50, 9:00-11:41
-"Mosuo." *Wikipedia.* references 10, 13, 22. last edited Sept 11, 2023.
https://en.wikipedia.org/wiki/Mosuo

[3]Schwartz, Realm of Women. 5:52.

[4]Schwartz, Realm of Women. 7:20, 7:18, 18:37.

[5]Wikipedia, Mosuo. 13.

[6]Schwartz, Realm of Women. 29:12.

[7]-Schwartz, Realm of Women.
-Kingdom of Women2, 31:00, 34:20, 34:29.

[8]Wikipedia, Mosuo. 13, 14.

[9]Wikipedia, Mosuo. 10, 12.

[10]Schwartz, Realm of Women. 33:00-33:30.

[11]-Wikipedia, Mosuo. 10, 12, 24.
-Schwartz, Realm of Women.

[12]Wikipedia, Mosuo. 5, 7, 10.

[13]Schwartz, Realm of Women. 34:09, 14:15.

[14]Wikipedia, Mosuo. 10, 17, 22, 23.

[15]"Top 10 Societies Where Women Rule." *YouTube Top 10 Archive*. 2021. https://youtu.be/wiLepgC9M7c

[16]Kingdom of Women2.

[17]Larsson, Milene. "The Land Where Women Rule: Inside China's Last Matriarchy." *YouTube*. *BROADLY. VICE Asia Production*. Feb 2016. https://www.youtube.com/watch?v=qMTJt2RnJAk

THREE DESTINIES

SURVIVAL OF THE USEFUL: ICE AGE TIPS

[1]Ayed, Nahlah (host) with Nowell, April. "Why it's important to learn how children lived in the last ice age: Lessons about how paleolithic children learned can carry lessons for our own parenting, say archeologists." *CBC Radio Ideas*. Updated July 18, 2022. https://www.cbc.ca/radio/ideas/why-it-s-important-to-learn-how-children-lived-in-the-last- ice-age-1.6371371

[2]*Connecting – Resilience – Indigenous Truth & Reconciliation: 'CRITR' Workbook*. P4. Grade 8-12, Education & Strength. Surrey: Classroom Ready Inc. 2022.

ACADEMIC-ACTIVIST-ARTIST

[1]"Research Week - Jeannette Armstrong." Video 1. *YouTube. Celebrate Research 2013*. https://youtu.be/rEwP2sH6GGE/

[2]"Jeannette Armstrong works to protect Indigenous philosophies and oral Syilx stories." *UBC Okanagan News*. (Faculty Profile, People). Oct 6, 2021. https://news.ok.ubc.ca/2021/10/06/jeannette-armstrong-works-to-protect-indigenous philosophies-and-oral-syilx-stories/

[3]Henningson, Donna. "No time like the present." *Penticton Herald*. 1999.

[4]"Jeannette Armstrong – Educator." *Wikipedia*.
https://en.wikipedia.org/wiki/Jeannette_Armstrong

[5]Protect Indigenous philosophies.

[6]Armstrong, Jeannette. Grauer, Lally. MacArthur, Janet, eds. *Okanagan Women's Voices: Syilx and Settler Writing and Relations 1870s-1960s*. 2021/22. i, vi, viii, 1.

[7]Okanagan Women's Voices. 138.

[8]Okanagan Women's Voices. 14.

[9]Protect Indigenous philosophies.

[10]-Okanagan Women's Voices. background of editors, 461.
-Janmohamed, Iman. July 24, 2023. "'We have our own voice': Dr. Jeannette Armstrong is a storyteller at heart." *The Ubyssey*. https://www.ubyssey.ca/features/our-campus-jeannette-armstrong/

[11]-Joseph, Things About Indian Act. 98, 20.
-"Haudenosaunee or Iroquois?" *New York State Department of Education* / New York State Museum (NYSM).
https://www.nysm.nysed.gov/education/videos/haudenosaunee-or-iroquois

-Ramsden, Peter G. (updated by Parrott, Zach). "Haudenosaunee (Iroquois)." *The Canadian Encyclopedia.* Dec 14, 2006. Last edit May 18, 2021. https://www.thecanadianencyclopedia.ca/en/article/iroquois

MARKETPLACE MOJO: TALL AGAIN IN THE SADDLE

[1]Louie, Clarence. *Rez Rules: My indictment of Canada's and America's systemic racism against Indigenous Peoples.* Toronto: McClelland & Stewart. 2021. p181.

[2]Louie, Rez Rules. 16, 322, front flap.

[3]Louie, Rez Rules. 14-16, 132, 150.

[4]Louie, Rez Rules. 209, 213.

[5]Louie, Rez Rules. 2, 162.

[6]Joseph, Things About Indian Act. 119-121.

[7]Joseph, Things About Indian Act. 70, 73.

[8]-Joseph, Things About Indian Act. 9.

  -Louie, Rez Rules. 217-218, 227.

[9]Louie, Rez Rules. 281, 292, 224, 278, 212.

[10]Louie, Rez Rules. 82.

[11]Louie, Rez Rules. 71-72, 232.

[12]Louie, Rez Rules. back flap.

[13]-Joseph, Things About Indian Act. 52.

  -Friends Schools in Kenya.

MOJAG HIJINKS WITH JUSTIN AND JODY

[1]"Jody Wilson-Raybould's father tells Pierre Trudeau his daughter wants to be PM." *YouTube.* CBC News. 1983. https://youtube/vhPnnLK6Znc

[2]Wilson-Raybould, Jody. *"Indian" in the Cabinet: Speaking Truth to Power.* p78, inside backflap. Toronto: HarperCollins. 2021.

[3]"Jody Wilson-Raybould." *Wikipedia.* https://en.wikipedia.org/wiki/Jody_Wilson-Raybould

  -Wilson-Raybould, Cabinet. 142.

[4]Wilson-Raybould, Cabinet. 145, 164-5, 167, 47.

[5]Wilson-Raybould, Cabinet. 159, 203-4.

[6]Swain, Diana. "An economic reality check on SNC-Lavalin: Are 9,000 jobs really at stake?" *CBC News. Business.* Updated Mar 9, 2019. https://www.cbc.ca/news/business/snc-lavalin-scandal-economics-jobs-risk-1.5047248

[7]Wilson-Raybould, Cabinet. 210-12, 215.

[8]Wilson-Raybould, Cabinet. 212, 240

  -Swain, SNC-Lavalin.

[9]Wilson-Raybould, Cabinet. 146, 153. (*See* Further Notes.)

[10]Wilson-Raybould, Cabinet. 178, 181, 295.

[11]Wikipedia.

[12]"COP26: Obama tells young people to stay angry on climate fight." *BBC News*. (*See* Further Notes.) Nov 8, 2021. https://www.bbc.com/news/science-environment-59210395

[13]-Brush Dance Mindful Living (2015 calendar). Seneca quote (January). www.brushdance.com
-"Seneca." *Brittanica*. https://www.britannica.com/biography/
Lucius-Annaeus-Seneca-Roman-philosopher-and-statesman

CHAPTER THREE – EVERYDAY AGGRAVATION

THE BIG "TRY" – WALKING THEM IN

[1]*Ironman Canada Penticton*. 2023. https://www.ironman.com/im-canada

[2]"Mark" (pseudonym). Personal communication. August 29, 2022.

TEACHER RUMBLE

[1]Stone, Douglas; Patton, Bruce; Heen, Sheila. Harvard Negotiation Project. *Difficult Conversations: How to discuss what matters most*. New York: Penguin Books. 2010. (p220. Concept of a conversation coach.)

[2]Evenson, Renee. *Powerful Phrases for Dealing with Difficult People: over 325 ready-to-use words and phrases for working with challenging personalities*. HarperCollins Leadership. 2014. (p10-13)

[3]Evanson, Powerful Phrases. 51-63.

[4]Evenson, Powerful Phrases. 31-33.

[5]Evenson, Powerful Phrases. 69, Chapter 5.

[6]"Fauci." *National Geographic Documentary Films. Disney Plus*. Sept 10, 2021.
https://www.disneyplus.com/en-ca

[7]"Fauci," National Geographic.

[8]"Fauci," National Geographic.
-"fauci." *Definitions*. https://www.definitions.net/definition/fauci

GRAND TOUR

[1]Grand Tour. *Wikipedia*. https://en.wikipedia.org/wiki/Grand_Tour. (*See* Further Notes)

SPORTS, SLAPS, AND FEELING LIKE A WOMAN

[1]-Troy Media. "Will Smith Slapped Chris Rock At The Oscars. Uncensored." *YouTube*. 2022.
https://www.youtube.com/watch?v=6sJz0xTiyiY
-Herbert, Steven and NBCLA Staff. "How Many Viewers Watched the Oscars After the Will Smith Slap?" Updated March 28, 2022. 8:53 pm.
https://www.nbclosangeles.com/entertainment/entertainment-news/oscars-2022-rises-will-smith-slap-chris-rock/2857982

[2]-"Will Smith – Chris Rock Slapping Incident." *Wikipedia*. Last edit Oct 5, 2023.
https://en.m.wikipedia.org/wiki/Will-Smith

-Kotb, Hoda. "EXCLUSIVE: Jada Pinkett Smith reveals she and Will Smith have been separated since 2016." *YouTube. TODAY. NBC News Exclusive.* Oct 11, 2023. https://www.youtube.com/watch?v=4O8qJNQurQ0

[3]Uncensored.

[4]-Juneau, Jen. "Chris Rock Appears to Call Will Smith's Recorded Apology a 'Hostage Video' in Comedy Set: Report." *People* Sept 2, 2022.

https://people.com/movies/chris-rock-appears-to-call-will-smith-apology-a-hostage-video-in-comedy-set/

-"Chris Rock slaps back at Will Smith in new Netflix special Chris Rock: Selective Outrage marked Netflix's 1st foray into live streaming." *CBC News. The Associated Press.* Updated Mar 5, 2023.

https://www.cbc.ca/news/entertainment/chris-rock-will-smith-netflix-live-special-1.6768766

[5]-"Germaine Greer." *Wikipedia.* Sept 20, 2023. https://en.wikipedia.org/wiki/Germaine_Greer

-"Gender-affirming surgery (male to female)." *Wikipedia.* Oct 2, 2023.

https://en.wikipedia.org/wiki/Gender-affirming_surgery_(male-to-female)

-Non-binary person (anonymous). Personal communication. November 20, 2023.

[6]"Germaine Greer: Transgender are 'not women' – BBC Newsnight." *YouTube.* BBC. Interview conducted by Kirsty Wark. 6:43. Oct 23, 2015.

https://www.youtube.com/watch?v=7B8Q6D4a6TM

[7]BBC Newsnight. Not women.

[8]Wahlquist, Calla. "Germaine Greer tells Q&A her trans views were wrong, but then restates them." *The Guardian.* Apr 11, 2016.

https://www.theguardian.com/books/2016/apr/12/

germaine-greer-tells-qa-her-trans-views- were-wrong-but-then-restates-them

[9]Intersex. "Common acronyms used within the Government of Canada."

https://women-gender-equality.canada.ca/en/free-to-be-me-2slgbtqi-plus-glossary.html-non-binary person, Nov 20, 2023.

[10]-Common acronyms, homosexual (no longer commonly used in English).

-Lyons, Kate. "I think Germaine Greer is wrong on trans issues – but banning her isn't the answer." *The Guardian.* Oct 27, 2015.

https://www.theguardian.com/commentisfree/2015/oct/27/

germaine-greer-transphobia- cardiff-feminism-inclusive

- Styles, Rhyannon. Team ELLE. "A trans woman's reply to Germaine Greer: ELLE's trans columnist Rhyannon Styles: 'Censoring her is not the right thing to do.'" *ELLE* Oct 27 2015. https://www.elle.com/uk/life-and-culture/news/a28166/a-trans-womans-reply-to-germaine-greer/

[11]Lyons, Wrong on Trans Issues.

[12]Non-binary person, Nov 20, 2023.

[13]Lyons, Wrong on Trans Issues.

[14]Lyons, Wrong on Trans Issues.

[15]TERF. June 15, 2018. *www.dictionary.com* https:///www.dictionary.com/e/gender-sexuality/terf/

PART TWO – MIND, EMOTION & SPIRIT

"TIP TALK" FORUM

[1]"What is a Gantt Chart? How to Use Gantt Charts in Project Management (with Examples)." *TeamGantt*. 2023. https://www.teamgantt.com/what-is-a-gantt-chart

CHAPTER ONE – MIND

FLOWERED DRESS: CAN I TRUST YOU?

[1]Louie, Rez Rules. 69.

-Giridharadas, Anand. *The Persuaders: At the front lines of the fight for hearts, minds, and Democracy*. Random House Audio. Oct 18, 2022.

[2]McRaney, David. *How Minds Change: The Surprising Science of Belief, Opinion, and Persuasion*. Portfolio. Penguin Random House. 2022. (p156, 165, 176)

[3]LBJ Foundation. "Civil Rights Summit: President Jimmy Carter's Emotional Tale about the Camp David Peace Accords." 1:40. *YouTube*. April 9, 2014. https://www.youtube.com/watch?v=l2b1ABQpKll

[4]McRaney, How Minds Change. xviii, xx, 222, 224, 238, 240

[5]Carter Center. "Our Mission." *Carter Center*. 2023. https://www.cartercenter.org/about/index.html

[6]Carter, Jimmy. "Camp David Accords: Egyptian-Israeli History." *Encyclopedia Brittanica*. Last updated April 19, 2023. https://www.britannica.com/event/Camp-David-Accords

[7]McRaney, How Minds Change. xiv, 195-6, 199.

[8]McRaney, How Minds Change. 30-33, 143, 227.

[9]McRaney, How Minds Change. 33, 35.

[10]McRaney, How Minds Change. 164-5.

[11]McRaney, How Minds Change. 166, 169.

[12]McRaney, How Minds Change. 60, 64, 69, 72-3, xviii-xix, 87, 257, 291

[13]McRaney, How Minds Change. 187.

[14]McRaney, How Minds Change. 109-111, 116-120, 284.

SILKY: YOUTH MEETS AGE-OLD WISDOM

[1]Schirch, Lisa and Campt, David. "The Little Book of Dialogue for Difficult Subjects." *The Little Books of Justice & Peacebuilding*. Good Books. New York: Skyhorse Publishing. 2007. (p8, 26)(*See Further Notes*)

[2]*Outlander*. season 4, episode 3. 3:17 (Scottish toast spoken by character Roger).

[3]-Metz, Thaddeus. "What Archbishop Tutu's ubuntu credo teaches the world about justice and harmony." Updated Oct 7, 2021. *The Conversation*. https://theconversation.com/what-archbishop-tutus-ubuntu-credo-teaches-the-world-about-justice-and-harmony-84730

- Evans, Katherine and Vaandering, Dorothy. "Little Book of Restorative Justice in Education: Fostering Responsibility, Healing, and Hope in Schools." *The Little Books of*

Justice & Peacebuilding. Good Books. New York: Skyhorse Publishing. Revised and updated. 2022. (p80)

[4]-"Kumbaya" (Kumbayah). Slang Dictionary. *Dictionary.com.* Mar 1, 2018. https://www.dictionary.com/e/slang/kumbaya/ accessed Feb 10, 2023.
-Slang Dictionary.
-Schirch/Campt. Difficult Subjects. 67, 78.

[5]-"The Four-Way Test." Guiding Principles. My Rotary. *Rotary International.* 2023. https://my.rotary.org/en/guiding-principles
-Legge, Done Fighting. Personal communication. Oct 12, 2023.

[6]-Evans/ Vaandering, Hope in Schools. 34.
-Zehr, Howard. "The Little Book of Restorative Justice." *The Little Books of Justice & Peacebuilding.* Good Books. New York: Skyhorse Publishing. 2015. Revised and updated. (p35)
-Schirch/Campt. Difficult Subjects. 79.

[7]Legge, Done Fighting. 274.

[8]Legge, Done Fighting. personal communication. April 21, 2022.

[9]-Legge, Done Fighting. 175, 176, 180.
-Schirch/Campt, Difficult Subjects. 26.
-Evans/Vaandering, Hope in Schools.
-Pranis, Kay. "The Little Book of Circle Processes: A New/Old Approach to Peacemaking." *The Little Books of Justice & Peacebuilding.* Good Books. New York: Skyhorse Publishing. 2005.
-Zehr, Restorative Justice.

[10]-Zehr, Restorative Justice. 14, 15
-Schirch/Campt, Difficult Subjects. 64.

[11]Evans/Vaandering, Hope in Schools. 39, 42-3, 73-4, 80.

[12]-Evans/Vaandering, Hope in Schools. 70-1, 87, 103.
-Legge, Done Fighting. 267. workshop 2022.
-"Interrupting Bias: The PALS Approach." Insight 10. *The Program on InterGroup Relations.* University of Michigan. Igr.umich.edu / IGR.Info@umich.edu
-Schirch/Campt, Difficult Subjects. 47, 41.
-Zehr, Restorative Justice. 45, 49, 51.

CHAPTER TWO – EMOTION

LEADERSHIP AND COURAGE: THE EMOTIONAL CLIFF

[1]Marquet, David Louis. *Turn Your Ship Around! A workbook for implementing intent-based leadership in your organization.* New York: Portfolio/Penguin 2015. (19, 78, 85, 90, 105, 111, 127, 133, 163, 169, 171, 175)

[2]Brown, Brene. *Dare To Lead: Brave work. Tough conversations. Whole hearts.* New York: Random House. 2018. (p41-42)

[3]McRaney, How Minds Change.

[4]Brown, Dare To Lead. 64-5.

[5]-Brown, Dare To Lead. Xiv.

-Clear, James. *Atomic Habits: An Easy & Proven Way to Build Good Habits & Break Bad Ones.* Avery/Penguin Random House. 2018. (front flap)

[6]-Brown, Dare To Lead. 4, 11, 15, 31-2, 38-40, 49, 57, 66-68.

-Prince Harry, The Duke of Essex. *Spare.* Random House Audio. Jan 2023.

-"Harry and Meghan." *Netflix.* 2022

-Personal communication (anonymous). October 25, 2023.

[7]Personal communication (anonymous). October 25, 2023.

[8]Brown, Dare To Lead. 73-4.

[9]Brown, Dare To Lead. 129, 134, 136, 143, 145-6, 148, 162, 167, 169, 176.

[10]-Whitlock, Craig. *The Afghanistan Papers.* Simon and Schuster Audio. Aug 2021. (Chapter two. p65-6)

-Brown, Dare To Lead. 201, 227, 187-190, 197.

-"Cuban missile crisis. International crisis. 1962." Mar 29, 2023. *Encyclopaedia Britannica.* https://www.britannica.com/event/Cuban-missile-crisis

-"Monroe Doctrine: American History." Last update Apr 4, 2023. *Encyclopaedia Britannica.*-https://www.britannica.com/event/Monroe-Doctrine

-Mearsheimer, John. "Why is Ukraine the West's Fault?" Uncommon Core: The Causes and Consequences of the Ukraine Crisis. *YouTube.* University of Chicago. 2015. https://www.youtube.com/watch?v=JrMiSQAGOS4

-"John Mearsheimer's inconvenient context: Who is responsible for this 'catastrophic war'?" *World Tribune.* Mar 8, 2022. https://www.worldtribune.com/john-mearsheimers-inconvenient-context-who-is-responsible-for-this-catastrophic-war/

[11]Brown, Dare To Lead. 196, 198-202, 210-11, 215.

[12]Brown, Dare To Lead. 224, 227-8, 230.

[13]Brown, Dare To Lead. 240, 242-3, 247, 251, 258, 265, 268, 270, 272.

CHAPTER THREE – SPIRIT

CONFIDENCE IN INNER SPIRIT

[1]Brown, Dare To Lead. 166.

[2]Robbins, Tony. "Unleashing The Power Within: Where the Impossible Becomes Possible." Virtual seminar. Workbook. Mar 2022. *Robbins Research International.* (p35, 11)

[3]Robbins, Unleashing The Power. 18.

[4]Robbins, Unleashing The Power. 43-4, 47.

BIGGER THAN ME

[1]SearchQuotes. 2023. Accessed Oct 8, 2023.

https://www.searchquotes.com/quotation/
We_are_all_visitors_to_this_time%2C_this_place._We_are_just_passing_through._
Our_purpose_here_is_to_ob/18340/

[2]Williamson, Everyday Grace. 89-98.

[3]-Williamson, Everyday Grace. 96.

-Brown, Brene. *Rising Strong: how the ability to reset transforms the way we live, love, parent, and lead.* Random House. 2015 (Rumbling With Forgiveness, p149-154)

-Legge, Done Fighting. 208.

[4]Tara Westover: "You Can Love Someone & Still Choose to Say Goodbye." *YouTube.* SuperSoul Sunday. OWN. May 5, 2019. Accessed Oct 8, 2023. https://youtu.be/BS0P1ovlRos

[5]Williamson, Everyday Grace. 97, 248-9.

[6]-Williamson, Everyday Grace. 58-9, 246-7, 163-7.

-Chopra. "Creating Peace From the Inside Out: The Power of Connecting (21-Day Meditations Experiences)". *YouTube.* Nov 21, 2021.

https://www.youtube.com/watch?v=RYWcaeTKX0k

[7]gr8light. "John Croft Dragon Dreaming Part 1 - Youtube." *YouTube.* Oct 2013. (*See* Further Notes.) https://www.youtube.com/watch?v=NdCL4DfGacI

[8]"Dragon Dreaming Project Design." Ebook. Version 2.09. 2020. (pinakarri, p9-10) https://dragondreaming.org/wpcontent/uploads/2020/01/DragonDreaming_eBook_english_V02.09.pdf

[9]dragon dreaming workshop. participant email. May 20, 2014.

[10]"Conflict in Quaker Meetings: Conflict or Opportunity?" Committee on Conflict Transformation. *Vimeo. New York Yearly Meeting of the Religious Society of Friends.* 2013. https://vimeo.com/82154625?embedded=false&source=video_title&owner=1589393

[11]"Addressing Conflict Amongst Friends." *Canadian Friends Service Committee (CFSC) / Continuing Meeting of Ministry and Counsel (CMMC).* Handout accessed Oct 8, 2023. https://quaker.ca/news/addressing-conflict-among-quakers/ (cover quote paraphrase, p2-6, 10-11, 13)

[12]Namaste: "The light within me honors the light within you." *karmicstones.com* https://karmicstones.com/products/namaste-the-light-within-me-honors-the-light-within-you

PART THREE – SPEAKING IN BLACK SWAN

BLACK SWAN SOARS

[1]Taleb, Nassim Nicholas. *The Black Swan: The Impact of the Highly Improbable. With a new section 'On Robustness and Fragility.'* Incerto Series. Random House. Second Edition 2010.

[2]Taleb, Swan. (About the Author)

[3]Taleb, Swan. (Prologue, Plum para8)

[4]Taleb, Swan. (Prologue, Plum para7)

[5]Taleb, Swan. (Prologue, Know para2-3; Suits para2)

[6]Taleb, Swan. (Prologue, Learn para2)

[7]Taleb, Swan. (Prologue, Bot para1; Unusual para2 + Nerd para4; Ingrat para3, 6)

AFTERWORD
[1]Marquet, L. David. *Leadership Is Language: The Hidden Power of What You Say – and What You Don't.* New York: Portfolio Penguin. 2020.

[2]Evans/Vaandering, Hope in Schools. 26, 47, 109

FURTHER NOTES:

FOUR GUYS
Smithfield, "Teddy Boys."

-1950s Teddy Boy style was Edwardian with a twist:

Ankle length tight pants, jackets a bit longer, white socks, vests sometimes brocade, skinny or western style tie, Oxford or suede shoes. Back-combed or slicked hair, with front curls. The look was a young John Lennon.

MOJAG HIJINKS WITH JUSTIN AND JODY
Wilson-Raybould, 146, 153.

-Jody Wilson-Raybould's proudest accomplishments in office include: the July 2017 creation of "Ten Principles Respecting the Government of Canada's Relationship with Indigenous Peoples," as well as a Working Group of Ministers, and a directive on how Wilson-Raybould's Ministry of Justice handled court cases regarding Indigenous rights.

BBC NEWS. COP26:Obama.

-QUOTE: "The thing we have going for us is that humanity has done hard things before," he said, adding: "I believe we can do hard things again."

GRAND TOUR
Wikipedia, "Grand Tour."

-The term "Grand Tour" comes from a common trip through the art centres of Europe (ie Italy) during the 17th to early 19th centuries, mainly by upper-class young European men (often British). It focused on classical culture, and was considered an "educational rite of passage." The term is used in this book as a metaphor for the experience and insight Tyrone gained about family relations from his trip.

SILKY: YOUTH MEETS AGE-OLD WISDOM
Schirch/Campt, p26.

-Class and education levels present differences in how people "express their thoughts, emotions and spirit through words." (Also, this can be differences in experience, age, or language background.) Helpful to session leaders: group people according to similar level, and use group games, drawing.

BIGGER THAN ME

Croft, John. "A Framework for running outrageously successful Dragon Dreaming Sessions." Seminar Oct 2013. (Material from draft manuscript. Author permission Dec 28, 2023)

- "A project….is a process of engagement, a deep dialogue with the world…the way in which the individual heals their separation, fear, alienation or a controlling domination of or by the world. It requires a process of 'deep listening' if it is to be a true dialogue rather than a single managerial monologue. Deep listening [,] where silence is also a form of communication and you are aware of the Earth speaking and listening simultaneously."

Printed in the USA
CPSIA information can be obtained
at www.ICGtesting.com
CBHW030413301024
16599CB00050B/520